DEVELOPING A RELATIONAL MODEL OF CARE FOR OLDER PEOPLE

by the same author

Ageing, Theology and Human Flourishing
James Woodward
ISBN 978 1 78592 314 2
eISBN 978 1 78450 626 1

of related interest

The Spiritual Dimension of Ageing, Second Edition
Elizabeth MacKinlay
ISBN 978 1 78592 072 1
eISBN 978 1 78450 333 8

Moving into Residential Care
A Practical Guide for Older People and Their Families
Colleen Doyle and Gail Roberts
ISBN 978 1 78592 189 6
eISBN 978 1 78450 462 5

DEVELOPING a RELATIONAL MODEL of CARE for OLDER PEOPLE

Creating Environments for Shared Living

JAMES WOODWARD and
JENNY KARTUPELIS

Jessica Kingsley *Publishers*
London and Philadelphia

First published in 2018
by Jessica Kingsley Publishers
73 Collier Street
London N1 9BE, UK
and
400 Market Street, Suite 400
Philadelphia, PA 19106, USA

www.jkp.com

Front cover image source: iStockphoto®. The cover image is for illustrative purposes only, and any person featuring is a model.

Library of Congress Cataloging in Publication Data
A CIP catalog record for this book is available from the Library of Congress

British Library Cataloguing in Publication Data
A CIP catalogue record for this book is available from the British Library

ISBN 978 1 78592 334 0
eISBN 978 1 78450 655 1

Printed and bound in Great Britain

MIX
Paper from responsible sources
FSC
www.fsc.org
FSC® C013056

Contents

Acknowledgements

The authors are very grateful to a number of people and organisations for all the help they have given in the development of this book.

First and foremost, thank you to Right Reverend Christopher Herbert, former Bishop of St Albans and Non-Executive Director of the Abbeyfield Society, currently Professor of Christian Ethics at the University of Surrey. Bishop Christopher's vision for sustaining and enhancing spiritual life in older age led to the commissioning of the study that has informed this book profoundly, and has stimulated the concept of relational care. He is an inspiration to all those he has encouraged and guided.

Our thanks to everyone at the Abbeyfield Society: those whom Jenny Kartupelis met during the study, who shared with her their thoughts, experiences and lives so generously and warmly; Paul Allen, Natasha Singarayer and Cameron Swift whose pioneering spirit enabled the study and its practical use; Anna Boyes, April Dobson, Teresa Gore and Edward Pogmore who advised on examples of new and good practice.

Our thanks to the community of the Foundation of Lady Katherine Leveson, Temple Balsall where as Master from 1998 to 2009 James nurtured a community of older people living in residential care and supported housing. Our thanks to Sarum College, of which James is principal, for providing a stimulating and enriching environment within which to research and write. The Centre for Human Flourishing in Sarum College will be the context within which further work will be done around age and ageing.

Our thanks to Natalie Watson at Jessica Kingsley Publishers, for having faith in us to write something that might be of use to all those involved in giving and receiving residential care.

Finally, but most heartfelt, are our thanks to our family, friends and colleagues who have borne with us when we have become a trifle obsessed about getting our ideas into type and reality; in particular, Trevor and John Kartupelis, Mark Pryce and especially for the inspiration of James's sister Colleen Parry and father Colin who continue to care for his mother, Patricia, at home.

INTRODUCTION

In this book two parallel narratives of professional engagement with age and social care are brought together through a shared interest in the nature of care for older people.

James Woodward has had a long-standing interest in pastoral theology and the nature of spiritual care since working at St Christopher's Hospice in south London as a nursing auxiliary from 1982 to 1983. Dame Cicely Saunders who founded the hospice has had a profoundly significant effect upon the reshaping of care at the end of life. This has and continues to be an inspiring influence on the thinking and practice of many who have experienced the quality of care in hospices and through the development of pain control.

This experience led James into healthcare chaplaincy (in Birmingham from 1990 through to 1996) and then into a charity providing housing for older people in an Almshouse Charity in Warwickshire. He established the Leveson Centre for the study of ageing, spirituality and social policy in 2000 and has continued to think about the nature and practice of age and ageing.

Jenny Kartupelis provides research, strategic planning and management services to interfaith and other charitable bodies, and was previously the Director of the East of England Faiths Council for 11 years, an organisation she helped to establish. The Council's main roles were to support local interfaith in the region, act as an advocate for faith in society and work with local and national government. Her professional background is in public relations and research, and it was this expertise that brought her into connection with the charitable work of the Abbeyfield Society, and she was commissioned to deliver a qualitative study about spiritual needs and care in Abbeyfield. In this respect, Jenny contacted James to talk through elements of this process; this conversation has continued and included the organisation of a consultation at St George's House, Windsor Castle, where James worked from 2008 to 2015.

These conversations have developed into a collaboration in the writing of this book. Both Jenny and James believe passionately in the possibilities that residential and supported care offer for older people. This book presents some of the findings of Jenny's research study together with a number of reflections about the nature of living together for older people, and we hope the insights will influence current policy and practice, indicating the societal value of a proven model of relational care.

The underlying assertions in this book are these: that we can again become committed to giving whole-person, loving care of the kind often previously provided by charities and religious communities for the indigent and old, but in a modern context; and that it is possible to reinvest, as a society, in collective living arrangements which provide a combination of supported private space with uninhibited access to the assurances provided by shared living. This stands against much of the recent trend to move away from the provision of residential care to offering support at home for older people.

The provision of care is uneven, and this has particularly been the case with those statutory and voluntary organisations that have provided residential and supported care. While we should remember what it is that many have disliked about residential living, we believe that living together in the right circumstances can be good, enriching and supportive for a fulfilled old age. In fact, it might be argued that our ambivalence about residential homes has much to do with a society that fails to value ageing and thereby seeks to marginalise and devalue this growing number of women and men across our families and communities.

Central to Jenny's research has been the discovery that for numerous reasons related to their own histories – their understanding, being and spirituality, coupled with some significant economic and financial constraints – some people benefit significantly from collective living. We should recognise that most people, for most of their lives, thrive from contact with others, indeed can become who they want to be through such interaction. Others, or maybe the same people, will want loving assistance in managing their lives – indeed defining the best of the misunderstood concept of 'asylum': sanctuary, peace, acceptance and support.

Living with others in a place designed to provide housing and loving service means living in an institution, and we use the word 'institution' in the neutral sense of an organisation and its building. We should escape from the platitudes and from polarised and even distorted social science and economics to the important questions. We should especially escape from the 'live at home or in a home' duality with the assumption that 'at home' is good and 'in a home' is an indication of sadness and failure, considering the ways in which people at different stages may choose to live with others. We need to have a much more energetic and informed conversation and review of the range of living arrangements which best suit numbers of people who want and may thrive on giving and taking support from others.

We hope that this contribution to the ongoing consideration of where older people should live and how they might live together will inform the search for an understanding of what makes some living arrangements satisfactory (even good) and others awful. Society must free itself from the policy drivers that insist that home is best, challenging as we do so the societal attitudes that demand inappropriate, impossible self-sufficiency and a particular type of 'independence'.

In this consideration, we should recognise the complexities and indeed the seemingly contradictory forces at play:

- We want to be by ourselves, and we want to be with others.
- We want to be self-focused, and other-focused.
- We want to do things for others and, forgetting others, to concentrate on ourselves.
- We want help and support, and we want to manage on our own, not being 'a bother'.
- We want our own place, and we want to share.
- We want to live with others around us and feel part of life, and we want to live on our own.

Solutions in social policy terms are not to be found solely in making residential homes or 'retirement villages' a fashionable alternative for those who can afford their fee levels. Perhaps the best answers will be found in allowing for different combinations of contact with others, indeed encouraging different groups of people to develop solutions that suit them and their communities, whether geographical or communities of interest. We acknowledge that such solutions must not be available only for the wealthy and the powerful.

In short, how can we construct places with spaces that nurture loving kindness to older people and through them offer their families and the wider community a quality of connection and relationship? We hope that this book stimulates further debate and action in developing new and improved relational structures and models for care.

CHAPTER 1

OLD AGE TODAY?
Setting the Scene

Introduction

This chapter begins with two narratives that set the scene as we begin to explore what kind of environment might best help an individual flourish in old age.

The use of experiences is deliberate. Too much of our social policy and cultural attitudes are removed from some of the dimensions of our own intellectual and emotional world. We seem resistant to engaging in an agenda of social change that might improve and develop the quality of life for older people, for reasons that may not be valid or evidenced.

The chapter examines the significance of demographic statistics before identifying some questions and issues raised by an ageing society. It then looks at the challenges posed to older people in living a healthy, engaged and dignified old age. It moves on to discuss the much-contested issue of how best to organise society to deal with the economics of health and social care in later life. In the final section, we shall look at the possibilities of re-imagining old age, acknowledging both the blessing and burden of ageing.

This will complete an overview offering a framework within which we can present and examine the research findings, their implications for the structures and shape of care in old age, and the vital role of personal relationships.

Listening to others and ourselves

JAYNE

Jayne is a 52-year-old librarian who has worked both here and abroad. She is single, independent and enjoys her freedom to choose and organise her professional and private life. She is an extrovert and enjoys keeping busy. The variety of jobs over her professional life has meant that she has never had one pension arrangement with a single employer, and she has tended not to think about any investment in the future through pension payments. She lives in a small flat in Leicester and appreciates easy accessibility to shops and other facilities.

Jayne has never considered what the next 30 years might look like for her especially in relation to her housing. She is resistant to considering what her choices might be and prefers not to think ahead especially when it might involve any consideration of her possible frailty or dependence.

SHARON AND MICHAEL

Michael is now 80 and is looking after his wife in the home that they have shared for the last 50 years. They have six children scattered across the country. Sharon, their eldest daughter, has given up her work to look after her mother and father. Sharon and Michael have lived with a slow progressive deterioration in their loved one, who is suffering from Alzheimer's. This took some time to diagnose and the support that they have had from the local GP and district nurses has been unpredictable and sometimes unsatisfactory. They have had three very traumatic experiences of hospitalisation in the local district general hospital where the care of their wife and mother was unsatisfactory and at times demeaning. Michael was adamant that none of the family should lodge a complaint about the way in which the hospital looked after his wife.

They are committed to all aspects of care at home including assistance with mobility, eating and personal care. This means broken nights and often periods of coping with distress, anxiety and confusion. The local care home has a bad reputation in the town where they live. They are resistant to exploring options around care elsewhere even though the stress of care is having an effect on their own wellbeing.

An ageing society: what are the facts?

Both globally and in the United Kingdom, we are experiencing a revolution in the opportunities that are offered by a steady increase in life expectancy. The statistics paint a picture that is translated into all kinds of practical realities.

In 2014 there were ten million people in the UK over 65 years old. By the year 2030, this figure is projected to rise to 15 million. By 2050, the number will have nearly doubled to around 20 million. Let us look at those projections from a different perspective: today almost one in ten people are over 60 years old; by 2050, one in five people will be over 60. By then, they will outnumber children aged 0–14.

These facts affect us all directly. A man born in the UK in 1981 had life expectancy at birth of 84 years. For a boy born today, the figure is 89 years, and by 2030 it is projected to be 91. The trend for women is similar. A girl born in 1981 was expected to live for 89 years and one born today might expect to live to 92. Projections suggest a girl born in 2030 might live to 95. We are all living longer and we should expect, in our families and communities, to have increased numbers of older people. There can be few of us who do not know friends or neighbours who are literally 'living with age'. Each of us will need to anticipate and prepare for living longer.

At this point it is important to bear in mind that the projection of accurate demographic figures is problematic due to variables in fertility and mortality rates. In some parts of the world, gaining accurate information can be difficult and some projections have been based on false assumptions. These variables all have implications for policy makers planning services for older people. However, within this total statistical picture, the number of very old people (over 85) grows even faster. This brings particular challenges to the debate about our provision for meeting their needs. Much of today's public spending on benefits is focused on elderly people: 65 per cent of Department for Work and Pensions benefit expenditure goes to those over working age, equivalent to £100 billion in 2010/11 or one-seventh of public expenditure.

Continuing to provide state benefits and pensions at today's average would mean additional spending of £10 billion a year for every additional one million people over working age.

Growing numbers of elderly people also have an impact on the NHS, where average spending on retired households is nearly double that for non-retired households: in 2007/08 the average value of NHS services for retired households was £5,200 compared with £2,800 for non-retired. These averages conceal variation across older age groups, with the cost of service provision for the most elderly likely to be much greater than for younger retired people. The Department of Health estimates that the average cost of providing hospital and community health services for a person aged 85 years or more is around three times greater than for a person aged 65 to 74 years.

It looks extremely likely that, in the coming decades, rapidly ageing populations will increasingly strain health, welfare and social insurance systems, putting potentially unsustainable pressure on public budgets.

Some issues raised by an ageing society

Reframing our relationship to time and work

Living longer offers us the chance to reframe our relationship to time and to the various stages of our living. We need to re-think what we believe about the nature of work and the relationship between paid and unpaid activity. Concepts of retirement have changed, with older people beyond 65 feeling that they still have a useful part to play in society. There are issues relating to family and the responsibility that the different generations have for one another, especially when older age presents health and social care challenges.

The consequences of an ageing population present society with major issues of public policy: critical questions that face both the voter and those seeking a mandate to govern. These questions are in part related to finance and are wide ranging. For example, who should be responsible for pensions and other income support? How do we provide the best health care for older people within the limitations set on NHS spending, particularly given the increase in those living with dementia-related conditions? Can the State always be expected to meet the needs and associated costs of social care? How and where should older people live and how innovative are we in the provision of suitable housing?

The physical and spiritual dimensions of growing older also present some real anxieties and fears. In an individualistic, consumerist and materialistic world, is it possible to affirm that we are blessed by the presence of older people? Indeed, as we face the prospects of ageing what are we to make of the negative images and stereotypes of old age? How far do these representations shape our sense of what age means or are we shaped by the denial of ageing in twenty-first-century Britain?

Transforming attitudes towards old age

What is needed is a fundamental change in how we as a society think and feel about old age. In other words, we should listen more carefully to the experiences of Jayne, Michael and Sharon, alongside our own. What might it mean to work towards human flourishing in our own old age and in the ageing of others? This is a core theme in our shared commitment to the nurture of the common good in our communities.

However, in order to realise this vision there will need to be some shifts in social, ethical, financial and political thinking to enable old age to fulfil its potential in us, and through us, in society.

What are the challenges that older people face?

Older age can bring a range of challenges to maintaining independence. These might include physical frailty, pain and cognitive issues. A small proportion of older people have to accept the need for help from relatives and neighbours. Some may need to have paid carers to help with basic tasks of living, while others may need to accept a transition into residential care. Age can bring with it some cognitive impairment and even dementia. These and other factors combine to make this age group vulnerable to isolation, depression and sometimes abuse and neglect.

Our experience has indicated that loneliness often besets many older people. This may be caused by the way in which an individual's social networks shrink. Family members, including children, may well live at a distance. Isolation may be the result of the death of a partner or indeed of children.

The context and culture within which ageing takes place are significant shaping influences for older people. Grandchildren are important for grandparents but often grand-parenting takes place at a distance or in the context of family breakdown. Older people can sometimes find it difficult to cope with the gaps and differences in values and ways of living (for example, the reliance on modern technology and social networking as part of keeping in touch). They may express their concerns, especially about the economic fortunes of their families, as all live with the reality of differences in property and income.

Ageing is also an inner journey as there are emotional, psychological and spiritual tasks to be faced. Older people need to come to terms with their lives as they reflect on its shape and fortunes, and there may be a need to face bad and often traumatic memories. There is infinite value in this process. The inner work done in later life can be the means by which the treasure of wisdom can be passed down to younger generations. There is a need for the elderly to consolidate their identity, which will include a healthy acknowledgement of mistakes and the aspiration to leave a legacy of something worthwhile after death.

Older adults, like people of all ages, will have to find their own way of dealing with death. Some may deny it, resisting at all costs any open conversation about understandable fears of living and dying alone. Some will even avoid any preparation for death that takes the shape of planning and paying for a funeral. There can be few, however, who do not wonder what shape their death might take and what chances there may be of dying with dignity. It remains our shared responsibility to embrace the realities of death through encouraging a more open approach to conversation, reflection and preparation for dying and death. This may also mean a clearer sense of what the choices and decisions are around the end of life.

Finally, we should not understate how the prevalence of negative attitudes towards older adults affects them. These attitudes include indifference (many older people feel invisible and unvalued), pity, resentment and fear, which could even lead to a stigmatising and stereotyping of mature adults as out of date, and at worst greedy and selfish.

Financial and political issues

The statistics that concern 'population ageing' give rise to a number of stories about increased longevity and often have a number of things in common – it is bad, it is new and it will overwhelm us all. The major fear is the burden of cost and caring that having greater numbers of older people in society will create.

We should note that 'population ageing' has been taking place for almost two centuries in the UK. We should also note the diversity of the ways in which people age and the interconnectedness of culture, economic status, housing, employment and the provision of health care. Some, though not all, would add that a person's spiritual and religious world also impacts significantly on how they age. It will be important to ensure that those who generate public policy include within their vision a holistic view of human personhood and the intrinsic value of all stages of living and dying as we seek to make the best provision for the common good.

In this context, far too much of the 'care debate' has concentrated on the important but rather narrow agenda of whether we shall be able to 'afford' ageing. This is a significant debate and still largely unresolved, and was little dealt with in the political debates during recent general elections.

We would do well to attend to the way this debate is conducted. In order to make choices, we need information. Too many of the conversations that take place about older people are simply inaccessible to the general public. The more politicised the discourse, the less we are able to negotiate the contested areas of policy. These debates (necessary as they are for democracy) often fail to place the issues into a broader and wiser historical and cultural horizon. To pick up the image of that man in the wing mirror of my car, we fail to make the connection between older people, the fabric of our lives and the prospects for our own ageing.

The Dilnot Report as a way forward for funding care

There have been a number of attempts to offer solutions to reform the funding of the care of older people. Recent discussion has focused on and around the proposals outlined in the Dilnot Report.

The Report's main findings were:

1. Public policy must face the fact that state expenditure in England on older people's social care is not keeping up with rising demand.

2. Care costs for any one individual are uncertain and can, in some circumstances, be very high indeed.

3. The current system of funding individual care in England, which requires people with more than a very modest level of capital assets to use those assets to cover the cost of their care, leaves many in fear and uncertainty as they approach one of the most vulnerable periods of their life.

4. A system is required for funding care that enables the risk to any one individual to be pooled, through taxation or insurance or, preferably, a mix of both. The Report proposes a system under which the individual will be responsible, on a means-tested basis, for the costs of his or her care up to a suggested level of £35,000, after which the State would pick up the cost. The current asset threshold for those in residential care would also be extended, from £23,250 to £100,000.

Such a system, the Report argues, will provide sufficient certainty to enable people to plan ahead, and allow the financial services industry to develop insurance and other products to help them with their planning. It will also help the poorest in our society the most.

The research underpinning the Report estimated the cost to the public purse of its proposals at less than £2 billion. While we continue to be in a time of some economic constraint, finding the funding for old age care will clearly not be easy. There will certainly be debate about the priorities for Government spending. But there is also a conversation to be had about the values that should undergird decisions made about the levels of tax necessary for the kind of society we wish to see, where all may flourish. In this debate we should remember that the £2 billion that Dilnot suggests would fund care is very modest compared with a total annual Government expenditure of just under £700 billion.

The persuasiveness of the argument about resource constraints should be viewed against the implications of not making this investment. One implication is that the cost of caring for older people already falling on the NHS and other parts of the national budget is likely to go on increasing. In other words, resistance or delay to the introduction of a fairer system of funding means that problems and pressures on the State provision will continue, not be avoided, and incur further unexpected and unplanned cost.

The Government has incorporated the 'cap on care costs' proposed in the Dilnot Report into the Care Bill (making its way through Parliament as I write). If passed, the cap would be set at a higher level (£72,000) but future governments would have the option to lower it should the fiscal climate improve, or indeed to raise it. The Care Bill also includes a proposal to raise the upper threshold for means-testing to £123,000. These steps have been welcomed as important, albeit not sufficient. As time passes, concerns are growing about the extent to which the changes will be experienced as an improvement, or whether the new system will be found as confusing and complex as the current one. Deliberations continue about fairer and more sustainable ways to fund health and social care – for example, in the context of the work of the independent Commission on the Future of Health and Social Care in England set up by the King's Fund and currently ongoing.

The Dilnot Commission also recommended other reforms, including a major information and advice campaign to help people plan; better information and needs assessment for carers; and better integration of health and social care. The aim of this approach to justice and human flourishing is to achieve the right balance between individual responsibility and publicly funded provision.

A new social contract is needed which – on the basis of an honest assessment of the respective roles of the State, voluntary associations and individual citizens – assures the weak and vulnerable of proper protection and gives all of us confidence that we are committed to building the conditions necessary to assist everyone to thrive.

The blessings and burdens of age

The discussion about the funding of care needs also to be put into the context of some of the organising narratives and possible misconceptions that shape the ways we look at age. Might we be able to hold together some of the burdens of older age with the opportunities and blessings of mature years? Longer life and increased numbers of older people result in many positive things for the community and our common life. In this part of the chapter we look at the defining of age; myths of dependency and health in old age; the relationship of poverty to old age; the pensions debate and the notion of retirement; and the perceived threat of dementia.

Redefining old age

We must be careful about the ways in which we frame how 'old' age is defined. There are many who are thankful for the possibility of living longer and view getting old as a good thing. We may actually relish the prospect of living longer. Age redefined might affirm that we are actually getting younger if you count the years we have left to live! A wider view of these statistics indicates that over time we can expect people of successive generations to be healthier and fitter and have longer to live at any age than their predecessors. This is a situation that could bring an abundance of opportunities and blessings.

An age in years that may be viewed as 'old' now may not seem so in 50 years' time. We shall need to redefine age in the light of this and look again at what we mean by old.

The exploration of a positive defining of age will have to contend with the reality that a great deal of our culture is frenetically oriented towards youth. This may be understandable: people want to put down markers for the future as they see it and to capture the attention of a younger generation. Nevertheless, it should be possible to hold together our perspectives of the generations in a way that does not ignore the reality of responsible, active people in older life, who are still participants in society, not passengers. Younger people forget that they are ageing themselves, and should play their part in planning for how we think about and prepare for older age. Younger people will be in need of positive and hopeful models for their own later years. We tolerate a very eccentric view of the good life, or the ideal life, as one that can be lived only for a few years, say, between 18 and 40. So the work of redefining age becomes critical if we want to break out of either wanting older citizens to go on as part of the productive machine for as long as possible or of giving in to an ageism that accords them a marginal and humiliating status, in which they become tolerated but not valued.

Are all older people dependent?

A key part of reframing our relationship to older age is to remind ourselves that most old people are not 'dependent'. For the first time, a million people aged 65 or over are still in paid work. Indeed, if we define dependency as 'not in paid work', then there are more dependents of 'working age' in the UK than there are people over state pension age who don't work. The number of people working past state retirement age has almost tripled over the past 15 years. A TUC survey showed that 258,000 women and 338,000 men are still working at the age of 65 and over, against 93,000 and 112,000 in 1998.

A great many older people report their health as good. At the time of the 2011 census there were about 300,000 people aged over 64 in care homes (including public and private, with or without nursing) – just over half a per cent of the population of England and Wales. Many of them are not dependent financially but are affluent and support younger family members.

Old age, poverty and pensions

We should not confuse old with poor. Those who are poor are rarely poor because they are old: they are poor now because they were poor when they were younger, unable either to accumulate assets or pension rights to draw on in later life.

Discussion of the economics of ageing is very often dominated by the concern that we cannot afford pensions. A little over a century ago, annual working hours in the UK were double what they are now (at around 3,000 hours per year). Working lives were also longer: boys and girls might leave school at 12 or 13, whereas now employment rates don't peak until the mid-20s as students leave higher education, and many retire from work before reaching the state pension age. The issue here is not that we cannot afford pensions but that the nature of work has changed and we need a different set of arrangements for pensions to reflect this.

Individuals retire at different ages and the present generation of people over 60 has the advantages of well-resourced pensions. Only those who have not accumulated the assets necessary to choose retirement will be forced to work on. The affluent will continue to be able to afford to retire early. Worst of all, it is those most likely to end up working up to the state pension age who will be least likely to survive to enjoy a long retirement. The poor, those in manual jobs or those living in areas of social deprivation have life expectancies five to ten years below their more privileged peers.

None of this means that older people shouldn't be encouraged to work longer – if that is what they choose to do. However, to suggest that an economy as productive as that of the UK 'cannot afford' to let its least affluent members leave work until they are 68 or 70 is quite mistaken. This is not about a policy driven by economic or demographic pressure but reflects the political debate about the place of the State and particularly the resourcing of the welfare state in a cash-limited economy.

The fear of dementia

One of the reasons that we have an ambiguous relationship with age and ageing is the fear of what shape old age might take in us. As the number of older people increases, there are few of us who do not know the effects dementia and related diseases have on individuals and their families. Definitions of dementia vary across time and place (at what point does the general weakening of cognitive function that accompanies 'normal' ageing cross the threshold to dementia?), but there is a close connection to age, and 'early onset' dementia is very rare.

As life expectancy increases, society must recognise that many older people will live with, and die with, dementia. It is anticipated that the number of people in the UK with dementia will double in the next 40 years (800,000 people with dementia in 2012; 1,000,000 in 2021; 1,700,000 in 2051).

If the dementia from which someone is suffering is mild and compatible with independent living, it has few implications. If it is severe, it has the potential rapidly to increase demand for social and health care.

What we really do not know is how the relationship between age and dementia prevalence is changing. The dream scenario is that longer lives also mean later dementia; the nightmare one is that longer lives come with a fixed relationship between age and dementia, so that a rapidly increasing proportion of the extra years in longer lives are spent with the condition. We do know of factors that appear to delay the age of dementia onset, including more mental, physical or social activity: something vibrant communities can provide. There have been a number of Government initiatives to address the increased number of people living with dementia. Our response to this threat to wellbeing will be critical in how we collaborate for a good and blessed old age.

The contribution of older people to intergenerational care

Despite the problems associated with ageing, there are many positive attitudes of respect, interest and compassion for older people based in our experience of them as heroic, sacrificial and wise. In communities across the country older people play an important part in sustaining the common good through (for example) volunteering, unpaid childcare and support of neighbours, and they often play a critical part in the care of older partners. Older people in faith and cultural communities are often carriers of memory, story and identity.

Grandparents are the most important source of childcare after parents themselves; more important than either public or private provision. Older people make an enormous contribution in so many ways to the common good of our families, communities, churches and other places of worship. It is not easy to calculate with accuracy the net contribution of older people to the common good of societies. Figures from the United Nations (UN) show, from a global perspective, that more than 70 per cent of men and nearly 40 per cent of women over 60 continue to work. Age Concern UK published the following figures for unpaid care by older people in the UK (2010): three million unpaid carers (replacement value of £15 billion); grandparent care – one quarter of families use grandparent care each week (replacement value of £4 billion); volunteering – five million older volunteers (replacement value of £5 billion). This equates to a total value of £24 billion (equivalent to 3% of the economy).

There is one area that is particularly important – that of the intergenerational relationship. As family structures become looser and more scattered geographically, it is vital that there should be regular opportunities for interaction between younger and older people. As we explore what might make for a good community we shall need to address the ways in which the good of older people can be a practical part of the wellbeing of all people. Our vision must embrace the need to strengthen the bonds that bind all generations in our community together, especially at a time when these are under particular strain.

Conclusions

In this chapter, we have taken an overview of some of the issues that shape our present public debate about age and ageing in twenty-first-century Britain. It remains to be seen how far these questions might frame or shape the way people make democratic choices, but we must keep the human reality of older people to the forefront of our debates. In the choices that we make about how to provide for those most vulnerable in our communities, we must work across professional boundaries to provide the best care and support of older people. This book will develop the concept of person-centred care and argue that all care should in fact be relationship centred, and that wherever we live in older age the environment should be one that maintains health, independence and active life.

The rising numbers of older people living with dementia will make particular demands on mental health services. An older population will require a reconsideration of how communities and families organise for housing and both formal and informal care. These are economic issues about resources but also questions about how far the State can meet our expectations.

There will certainly need to be a change in attitude to inheritance, retirement and patterns of work. We shall need to ask ourselves about our responsibility for the vulnerable and poor older people in our society. These are issues of care and how we empower individuals, professionals and institutions to deliver better services for the sake of our communities.

At the beginning of this chapter we shared a lesson in the importance of recognising ageing in ourselves through others. This is about generating compassion shaped by imagination, which can help us to appreciate the true meaning and significance of ageing. Age can be a wise and challenging teacher. Older people can show how little time we give, in all our bureaucracy and busyness, to considering what substance and depth mean in being human. It is no accident that older people become more spiritual, and that they can help us to perceive that the process of ageing is a spiritual task.

This making of the soul takes shape when our human life is expressed in and through our stories. We need to value older people by listening to them. Their narratives need pondering, retelling, organising and appropriating. How might we, as communities and as a society, work together in moving age and older people and our responsibility to them further up the political agenda? How can those with the power to engage with ageism deal with the impoverishment of living that some older people face?

CHAPTER 2

THE SPIRITUAL LIFE OF OLDER PEOPLE

Listening to others

MICHAEL

I am sympathetic to religion. My parents were occasional churchgoers, and I attended a church school. I want to lead a good life but haven't found religion much practical help. I do not understand how to read the Bible and find some of the language of hymns and liturgy strange.

I taught Art in an inner-city comprehensive school for nearly 30 years – not the most popular of subjects in the school! It was a tremendous source of satisfaction for me when I could enable my pupils to express themselves and to appreciate the energy and imagination that artists can express. I often expressed my view that effective education could be achieved through 'pictures' as much as 'words'. Some of my happiest memories were taking pupils to the City Gallery and working with them to uncover the shape and depth and texture of a picture. I hope I shared with them something of how art can help us to see life and it possibilities.

In some ways I have always been on the edge of things – shy and introverted but a bit of a rebel. Most of my headteachers found me fairly unmanageable! Retirement came as a relief with plenty of time (and money) to pursue my painting and journey across European city art galleries.

I go to church from time to time, but as a single man I feel excluded by some of the talk of belonging and family. I am curious about the shape of meaning and the inner workings of a person's spirit or soul. I would appreciate the chance to reflect on these matters; to be listened to rather than talked at. I am told that older people become more spiritual as they age – I am beginning to want to reject this assertion – it doesn't bear out in my experience.

HELEN

I shall be 84 in April, so I have well exceeded the biblical three score years and ten. Every day, therefore, is a bonus 'something given above what is due'.

As I get older, I feel increasing cause for celebration in the seasons. Indeed, creation has an added significance year by year. Seemingly simple things take on an added meaning, for example, the bird table, the ever-changing trees, the bowls of spring bulbs, enjoyment we can share with other people.

One can take the enjoyment of the world on to a much more mundane level. Like many older people, I find that much more of my life is involved in domesticity. Here I am very blessed because my husband and I are able to work in partnership. I now look on cooking as a creative process as I am handling created things, the lovely colours and textures and shapes of fruit and vegetables, for instance.

We desperately want to hold on to our belief in prayer, but we are often embarrassed by our own inadequacy. I regard prayer as being an important responsibility and privilege in old age when I have more time and more experience than in the past. But I think that by now I should be better at it, and it is not easy to admit that. Physical health varies and spiritual health is just the same. Times of spiritual depression come to most of us. Sometimes it is linked with an inability to forgive. We all know the costliness of forgiveness and that coming to terms with it can be an important part of the unfinished business with which an elderly person can be struggling. There are now two aspects, forgiving and being forgiven. We have all been hurt; we have all hurt other people. In the Lord's Prayer, we say 'forgive us our trespasses as we forgive those who trespass against us'. I meet many old people who still live adventurously. But it is hard to be adventurous all the time, and the temptation can be there to give up because it is all too much of an effort now, and we can't change the world as we thought we could when we were younger. But even though we are limited by age, we can still make a difference. We can pray; we can keep ourselves informed; we can collect paper to help the environment; we can write to our MP.

Throughout life, we need a sense of humour, and perhaps, more so in old age when there are inevitable difficulties. I have noticed that in some old people a sense of humour seems to diminish and that is a real loss. It helps to have a companion with whom one can share a joke, so old people living alone may be disadvantaged in this respect. When we are old, we tend to make stupid little mistakes. Perhaps, for instance, we take longer to get coins out of our purse than we used to. This irritates us. It might be better if we responded in the spirit of the person who wrote, 'blessed are we who can laugh at ourselves, for we shall never cease to be amused'.

I have a certain amount of fear of the process of dying, but not death itself. In the case of death, we are all aware that we know so little about what happens after death. But if we trust God and His love for us, as far as I am concerned, I can feel secure, even though I do not know what form life after death will take.

As I have found in my personal experience, old age has drawbacks, but it also has strengths, one of which is a quality of detachment that leads to a sense of perspective. That will help, but it will not take away the darkness altogether, far from it. For example, old people in particular feel very let down by world affairs, including September 11th and all that it symbolises. Yes, we had to agree that the world was a wicked place, but we thought that on the whole there was some improvement. And now we seem to have encountered a new intensity of darkness.

I try to hold on to the words said to have been scrawled on a wall by a Jewish lad in prison in the 1940s:

I believe in the sun even when it is not shining,

I believe in love even when I cannot feel it,

I believe in God even when He is silent.

> I claim that for me a prayer attributed to Reinhold Niebuhr is particularly appropriate in old age. Here it is:
>
> > God grant me the serenity to accept the things I cannot change,
> >
> > Courage to change the things I can,
> >
> > And wisdom to know the difference.

We shall explore the concept of relationship-centred care in the subsequent chapters of this book. In this discussion we work on the assumption that the acknowledgement and meeting of non-physical needs of an older person are fundamental to their and societal wellbeing.

The purpose of this chapter is to explore some of the literature, definitions and practices surrounding the understanding of the spiritual life of older people. We should make it clear that throughout this chapter a distinction is made between spirituality and religion. They are indeed linked but our concept of relationship-centred care works on the assumption that we have some cognizance of the nature of the spiritual for an older person.

The concept of spirituality means many different things to different people and requires some unpacking and interpretation if there is to be any deeper understanding of expectations and needs: spirituality runs the danger of becoming a vague and diffuse notion, functioning like 'intellectual polyfilla', which changes shape and content conveniently to fill the space its user has devised for it.

For the purposes of this chapter we must note that many modern writers on this subject (by no means all of whom are care practitioners) regularly insist that spirituality is not the same as religion but refers to something much broader. The word spirituality, once chiefly used within a Christian setting for the understanding and practice of the devout life, has now widened its use in the light of modern circumstances. This understanding of the theory and practice of spirituality and spiritual care is certainly embedded in the present understanding of healthcare chaplaincy and its work but is also held by those working in palliative care. For example, Tom Gordon, working in Marie Curie Cancer Care, confidently asserts, 'we must understand the basic principles – that spirituality is common to all, and that it is not always synonymous with religion' (Gordon 1997).

Moffitt writes in an article entitled 'Helping to create a personal sacred space' that using the term spiritual 'frees us from being tied down to any one faith tradition' (Moffitt 1996).

Wilfred McSherry (2006) writing from a nursing perspective expands this point. He shows that spirituality is often viewed as being synonymous with religion and a belief in God. It follows that to adopt such a narrow definition is to exclude a multitude of people – atheist, agnostic, humanist – who may not share such beliefs, but who have a spirituality that is real.

So it follows that any reference to religion in common parlance will generally be understood to refer to its rules and regulations, rituals, beliefs and traditions, whereas usefully spirituality is understood as that which constitutes inner life or unseen workings – the forces and powers which propel it. This can be described as character and ethos, ideals and intangible beliefs which hold all together; even values and norms. Thus it follows that both individuals and particular organisations or cultures may have a spiritual character. Many have rejected the concept of spirituality precisely because it is so often used in the context of religious thinking and practice. Alyson Peberdy (1993) offers a simple distinction as she argues that we might see spirituality as a search for meaning, and religion as a particular expression of that and one that usually involves God-language.

In pastoral practice, however, it is much more problematic to separate spirituality from religion than these statements suggest.

Here is a list of the definitions of spirituality that have emerged from my work with health and social care professionals who seek to respond to an individual within the context of a holistic approach to support and care. Participants at workshops were asked to define what immediately came to their mind as a short definition of spirituality. These definitions emerged:

- Inner peace and wellbeing.
- Purpose.
- Love, warmth, understanding.
- Is incapable of definition.
- A dream or vision that gives meaning.

- A wholeness from within.
- Unconditional love for one another.
- Contentment.
- Being taken beyond oneself.
- Completeness.
- The searchings of the inner being.
- That which gives meaning and purpose to life.
- What matters most.
- Individual or unique value.
- Connectedness.
- Togetherness.
- Hope or faith.
- Relationship with God.
- Faith in inner self and religion.
- Communicating with God's spirit.
- Peace of mind.
- Satisfaction.

An overview of these definitions indicates a broad consensus around how spirituality may be sensed and thought of, and its inevitable connectedness with religion for those people whose spirituality has been shaped and nurtured in and through a faith tradition.

What are spiritual needs?

Travelbee offers this definition of spirituality: 'to assist individuals and families not just to cope with illness and suffering, but to find meaning in those experiences' (quoted in O'Brien 2011). Another doctor teaching medical students on a busy surgical unit offered this important insight in some personal correspondence:

> By teaching skills of knowing, hoping and trusting we should enable patients to trust experience or anticipate meaning. People need to make sense of their circumstances and to find a meaning in the events of their day, their relationships and their life.

Amidst this range of sometimes rather diverse definitions it is not surprising that when it comes to practice, many individuals and organisations have given up on the practice of spiritual care or have preferred to narrow the subject to its association with religion. This is particularly the case when considering the care and support of older people. In a busy and demanding day it is difficult for a care worker, charged to carry out a number of personal tasks for an older person, or indeed a friend or relative, to have any practical sense of how they might best respond to their non-physical needs. However, a good working definition of spiritual needs is vital, for it helps us to understand the integrating factor which can empower and facilitate good care. And, more basic, it helps us to keep this dimension of care firmly on the map.

There are five considerations implicit in the above, which might be summarised as follows:

- Addressing that which is inexpressible.
- Awareness of things greater.
- The sense of the transcendent that allows us to understand ourselves in context.
- What counts most.
- What helps us to make sense of life.

In this perspective, we can see that all of us are spiritual beings and that some of us express our spiritual needs through religion. This broad approach to spiritual needs and spiritual care affirms our inter-connectedness as whole people and acknowledges that our spiritual lives can often be under-developed in a reductionist and materialist culture – whether by our own neglect or by their deliberate suppression. For most of the older people that I have worked with there is some residual sense of the church and religion. If this volume is re-written for my generation in their third age in 20 or 30 years' time, this chapter will certainly take a very different shape. The capacity to find words to discuss the subject may simply have been lost.

The following three short extracts from writers best summarise this approach to spirituality:

> To care sometimes, to relieve often, to comfort always. (Anon)

> If I as a doctor spend an hour of my clinic time talking to a woman who has only a few weeks to live I am making a clear statement of her worth...I am affirming the worth of one individual person in a world in which the individual is at risk of being submerged or valued only for his strength, intellect or beauty... It is a prophetic statement about the unique value of the human person irrespective of their age, social class or productivity. (J. Woodward, personal communication 1998)

> As you ought not to attempt to cure the eyes without the head, or the head without the body, so neither ought you to attempt to cure the body without the soul...for the part can never be well unless the whole is well... And therefore, if the head and body are well, you must begin by curing the soul. (Plato)

In other words, spirituality, from this perspective, is about enhancing, enriching and expanding humanity. It embraces an ethical and social dimension as well as a person's opportunity or ability to be resilient in the face of change and disaster. It must also always have the older person as its focus and it must be committed, as we are in this book, to listening carefully to the diversity of experience that older people inevitably bring to those around them.

We need, all of us, to be more sensitive and imaginative about how we care for and learn with older people. This was brought out by a comment from a matron of a nursing home who, unable to be at the conference, wrote 'I am concerned about wanting to meet the spiritual needs of older people, many of whom do not ask or tell you what they want.' I think the comment characterises some of the difficulties in understanding and defining spiritual care, but it is also a spur for us to listen more carefully to older people. Evaluating and understanding an older person's non-physical needs can rarely be done in a short interview or assessment – it is a more radical, longer-term commitment to the person in all their mystery and richness.

There is much evidence to suggest that when people get older (beyond 55, to set a rather artificial marker) they do indeed become more open to the spiritual dimension of life. I have experienced some wonderment at the abundance of spiritual gifts so evident in people who are in their third and fourth age. It is my opinion that older persons are essentially faced with two choices: to turn in on themselves and the health problems that they may have, becoming set in their ways with fixed and relatively narrow patterns of thought; or, alternatively, to acquire a lifestyle based on openness to others, knowing how to welcome and understand partialness and difference and taking on board what is new. It is interesting to reflect in what way these choices are shaped by religion, culture, education and upbringing. Certainly, the person who chooses (if that is the right word) the lifestyle of openness has already learnt in earlier years how to grow old; this is someone who accepts and lives through this phase of life as a time of continuing growth, a process of evolution rather than involution. As an old man, George Bernard Shaw, affirmed: 'Physically I am declining but my mind is capable of growth because my curiosity is deeper than ever, my soul continues to march on' (Shaw 1939).

Paul Baudiqet, in his study of the artist Rembrandt and his paintings, concluded: 'Since his youth, Rembrandt had but one vocation – to grow old' (quoted in Nouwen 2003). Rembrandt had discovered early in his life the inner beauty that lay beneath the failing physical powers of older people. Much of his work consisted in portraying this in his graphic paintings of older people showing the depth of tenderness, serenity and inner strength that could still radiate through the gnarled hands and bent form of so many of his subjects. There was something about this inner life which attracted Rembrandt from his youth, showing him that the end time of life could be one of promise and fulfilment rather than despair and loss of dignity, even when it showed all the outward evidence of the latter.

There is an inevitable agony and ecstasy of the older person, which we need to attend to, listen to and learn from. The spirituality of ageing includes meeting and facing fear at an age when one is expected, or at least hopes, to be 'wise', 'settled' and 'integrated'. However, confrontation with and questioning of the ultimate meaning of life and death is, for some, an everyday experience –

and it brings with it wonder and fear, light and shadow, agony and ecstasy. This is no mere 'retirement' agenda, for it embraces life, time, experiences, memories, hurts, money, status, achievements. Life may become more simplified but it is also more focused. If older people pursue their search for meaning with intensity and support, so opportunities for spiritual development continue.

One might summarise spiritual needs, therefore, in the following ways. These needs are rooted in an understanding of spirituality as the way in which an individual responds to and makes sense of the raw experiences of life. They can be interpreted within or without a religious framework. There is a need in all of us:

- to feel valued and affirmed
- to love and to be loved
- to hope in something in this life and beyond
- to have faith and trust in someone or something
- to know peace, security and tranquillity.

We should note that spirituality is not a separate component of life and is not confined to moments of prayer and of conscious awareness of God or 'the other'. It underlies the whole of our lives – our aspirations, desires, fears and self-searching. It is the ground of our friendships, delight in nature and all creation, our relationships with others as well as God. These needs or longings or yearnings are satisfied in all kinds of ways and in all kinds of 'cathedrals'. For some, their essential spiritual needs are met through relationships and especially the family; for others through the satisfaction of consumerism; for others through sport and leisure and recreation. These diverse longings colour our aspirations and our hopes, our values and our choices. But like plant seeds, they need to be nurtured and sifted, so that the best are able to grow stronger and to blossom.

One of the opportunities that growing older gives us is to attend to this dimension of our life. From this perspective, one could argue that mature age is part of the all-wise and all-loving plan of our Creator and can hold within it special blessing. It is this blessing that older people are called to find and to celebrate; for these can be wisdom years. Life can be a journey towards wisdom, but it will not be complete until we come to terms with what Erickson calls 'the un-alterability of the past and the un-knowability of the future' (quoted in Wainwright 2001). This finds resonance with the four stages (or Ashramas) of life in Hinduism: the 'student' youth who is learning; the 'householder' who is devoted to family, work and duty; the 'retired' or hermitage stage with a return to contemplation; and finally the 'renunciation' when 'The person, now an elder full of wisdom, inwardly aims to renounce all the outer goals of life. He also becomes a teacher of the spiritual knowledge and no longer partakes in social or political concerns' (Frawley 1990. p.72).

In a somewhat different perspective, one might think in terms of a range of needs put like this:

- The need for community.
- The need to be needed.
- The need for celebration and laughter.
- The need for recognition of individuality.
- The need for acceptance.
- The need to be rather than to do.

Older people can become a reservoir of values to transmit to new generations. Experience has shown that wherever older people are valued, included and enabled to participate, the community is a richer one. For example, older people can show us that accepting limits is part of human life and there is a value in being rather than having and producing. Certainly, old age often brings with it losses; yet I have seen how older people with a number of medical conditions who were nonetheless positive about their state of health, lived longer than those, who, although being less ill, had a negative attitude towards the situation they were in. This shows that a person, even with a number of physical illnesses, can in reality be healthier than another, perhaps with none, if that person accepts their limits and sufferings, living out their condition as an opportunity for spiritual growth. Spiritual needs, which generally become more intense in older people, can become gifts in the context of reciprocal relationships.

It is the spirit of fraternity that makes us come out of isolation and weave a network of relationships in esteem and solidarity in which every stage of life can acquire a new understanding of its own beauty and at the same time of the beauty of the other. Sheila Cassidy (1989) reflects that it is the lavishing of precious resources, our precious ointment on the handicapped, those with mental illness, the rejected and the dying that most clearly reveals the love of Christ in our times. In her writing she argues that it is a particular form of Christian madness which seeks out the broken ones, people with dementia, the handicapped and the dying and places before their astonished eyes a banquet normally reserved for the whole and the productive.

So, we acknowledge that a person's spirituality manifests itself in a very wide variety of ways. It is a complex phenomenon shaped by many factors, touching as it does on fears and aspirations, hopes for life and reflections on death. It is deeply personal and, while some diagnostic or assessment tools can help appreciate a person's spiritual need, it is best quarried through ongoing relationship, conversation and trust.

There is a story of a woman who came across Michelangelo in his studio chipping away at a beautiful block of marble. Shocked by the waste as the pieces of marble piled up, she rebuked the sculptor. He looked at the stone and at her and then replied: 'The more the marble wastes, the more the statue grows.' This story reminds us that in addressing the spiritual needs of older people we should attempt to ensure that as the wasting takes place, older people are valued, and something of greater value is being allowed to grow.

I wonder sometimes why many people avoid deeper and more meaningful relationships with older people – something that happens at all kinds of levels. Carers can 'care' without engaging; worship can happen without engaging those taking part. Perhaps there is a part of us all that denies the ageing process and fears what older people represent. We need then to come to terms with the 'elderly stranger' within ourselves, to face our fears, and thereby free ourselves to respond, to listen, to learn and to grow in dignity towards our ultimate destiny.

CHAPTER 3

LISTENING TO THE VOICES OF OLDER PEOPLE

One of the points that emerge from the contextual overview in Chapter 1 is that in many senses the care of older people has become an industry. This is not surprising, given the numbers involved, and the requirements (sometimes valid) for 'professionalisation'. Yet it is clear that people should not, under any reasonable moral system, become commodities. More insidiously, there may be a danger of paying lip service to their humanity by the use of phrases such as 'person-centred' while making assumptions based, for example, on the evidence of those not receiving the care; on outdated notions; or on purely quantitative or unmediated qualitative data.

At the risk of stating the obvious, the best source of information on what older people require by way of 'care' is to ask those receiving it, or who feel they may imminently do so. Obvious, but in itself too simple, because it is beset by questions: which people, what are they to be asked and with what purpose, and given the likely divergence of response, what models may their answers indicate? Researchers the world over know that aspirations and realistic answers are not the same: a respondent asked if they would like a bus service from their front door direct to the shops and running every five minutes would eagerly assent; yet it would be logically impossible for them fully to use such a service.

So how are the voices of older people to be heard in such a way that decision-makers can understand more about what is perceived as a good quality of life, and the factors that are most relevant to that perception?

Snapshot: Freedom to be

Edith has lived a very full life: as a teacher, a mother, a Girl Guide leader and a musician. But she never had time to explore her wish to paint. Now she is an artist, taking lessons, painting and sketching the Suffolk countryside. Her small room is full of her work, and places have also been found for it in the corridors of the home she shares with eleven other older people. I do wonder if she finds her current accommodation rather claustrophobic, but two windows help, and she seems very settled. She tells me how happy she is to have discovered another side to herself: 'I'm a lady of leisure now…I'm as free as a bird.'

A good quality of life may be dependent on health, family, feelings of security, settled accommodation, good nutrition, lack of money worries and so on. These and many other factors may foster wellbeing, but do not in themselves make a life worth living. It is generally accepted that most people will look beyond these issues and talk about 'meaning' in their lives: a feeling of purpose, belonging or fulfilment. This is what the concept of 'spiritual wellbeing' encompasses and these profound matters are the most difficult to discuss in direct questioning and yet the least difficult to appreciate when they emerge in conversation.

Finding the right questions and the right time and environment to truly listen – that is, to become a channel of communication between the speaker and a wider audience – is more challenging than would appear at first thought. We are accustomed to interviewers asking questions with defined purposes: to gain material for media use; for a survey that has already set its own specific questions; as the basis of a planning or decision-making exercise.

This makes the concept of listening 'with purpose but without purposes' a delicate balance between meeting the needs of the speaker to be acknowledged in their own right and the needs of the listener to interpret and disseminate what they believe they have learnt. It is like having a butterfly settle on one's shoulder:

give it direct attention, and it will take flight. One has to appreciate it out of the corner of the eye.

And so it is with talking to older people and their carers about the elusive butterfly of spirituality. However, this is not an argument in favour of just sitting over cups of tea and biscuits, with no purpose in mind. Indeed, that could imply a lack of respect for the time and knowledge that people are willing to share. It is my experience that it is essential to use a semi-structured approach, with questions to guide and record the conversation, but never to dominate it. Those being interviewed want to understand the nature and purpose of the survey, even if they may be sceptical or indeed initially deterred by its focus on spirituality.

In 2014, I was invited by The Abbeyfield Society, a charity managing residential care homes and sheltered housing across the UK and beyond, to undertake a project investigating the nature of spiritual life in their homes. The questions that framed the work were: what constitutes spiritual care, what is its purpose, who should deliver it and how can it be delivered effectively?

The remit was wide: we were investigating how residents, staff and volunteers felt supported to live life as fully as possible, to find contentment and meaning in their past and present. As a charity with strongly Christian roots, Abbeyfield also wished to explore the significance of religious belief and practice in the lives of their homes. However, it was important that garnering information remained free of any assumptions about the presence or nature of the interviewee's faith convictions. Similarly, to achieve meaningful listening it was essential not to become too immersed in the academic and theological arguments about the nature of spirituality, but rather to keep returning to practical, critical questions: what do the people I am meeting feel about their lives, and what is happening around them that affects those feelings?

One of the factors that distinguished the Abbeyfield study was the decision to explore the responses and hence care of *everyone* in the community of the home, rather than to focus on the residents alone. Another was the extent of the study, with over 100 people being interviewed during its course, in a variety of geographical locations and different settings, from supported housing to care homes.

Snapshot: Scones have to be home-made

On the frosty morning of a January day, the Scottish hills look beautiful, and the more so for being viewed from behind a double-glazed window. Six ladies are seated at a round table, and the tea and home-made scones, courtesy of housekeeper Kirsty, could not look more tempting. Kirsty is showing us a photo of the wedding dress she will be wearing in May, and after a pause to appreciate the excitement, and ask more about plans for The Day, three of the ladies start to tell tales about their own weddings. Tales that are at least as funny as romantic. The others are quieter, perhaps enjoying memories, or maybe not all of them were married, or happily married at any rate. But there is a feeling of closeness. Later Kirsty says that the real conversations happen around the fire, when tea is served as dusk arrives. 'Or maybe a wee sherry – that always helps!'

Listening with purpose

Each site visit took between a half and a full day, and started with walking around, looking at the setting and facilities, and having informal conversations. Interviews of about one hour each then took place, normally in a private setting such as the manager's office. Residents chose whether to meet me in their own rooms, or a communal area; if the latter, we ensured that it could be private during the interview. I often stayed for lunch and chatted to people at the table.

Visits followed a format, such that data about homes (e.g. IT facilities, type of rooms) could be collected; respondents could be asked about specific themes and practices but they could also give any other information or opinions they wished. We designed a semi-structured questionnaire for interviews, but did not pose the questions sequentially, instead mapping the answers later into a standard form. This ensured that the entire meeting was captured as it happened, as a conversation rather than an interview.

After a small number of pilot interviews, the questionnaire was adapted to cover more about the physical environment, and some exploration of how staff changes impacted on wellbeing.

The focus was on listening and recording, and the function of the questionnaire (which interviewees were not given) was twofold: to ensure the main themes were covered, and to act as a prompt without interrupting the flow of conversation.

The selection of respondents was intended to give a wide range of voices, and to avoid self-selection whenever possible. So in the case of managers, staff and volunteers, it was the person who happened to be present on the day of the interview. This meant that occasionally there were interruptions when an issue demanded immediate attention, and this was in itself a learning opportunity: what type of matters arose during a normal day, and how did the relationships in the home affect the way in which they were dealt with? In the case of residents, managers chose people who were willing but not necessarily eager, and who had varying length of experience in a home. Some were long-standing and could give insights into the network of relationships, while other were recent arrivals, who could compare the setting with their previous place of abode.

The importance of a supplementary mode of 'listening' became clear during the study: the element of 'hearsay'. People would explain how other people in the home felt about their lives, using relayed conversations and anecdotes. This may be considered unsuitable to the conduct of pure research, but the essence of this study was about widening the net as much as possible, to capture feelings, perceptions, ideas and experience. Nothing was irrelevant. Taking this approach does mean that the 'listener' becomes part of the process, such that everyone involved co-creates the final report, and this in turn gives the greatest respect to the participants and allows their voices to be heard unimpeded by any narrow objectives or time constraints but mediated through synthesis and moderation to facilitate clearer or collective messages.

Sharing lives

An issue with this approach can be the expectations of those who take part. Initially, even after agreeing to do so, there can be suspicion; in the case of Abbeyfield, a number of people had strong reservations about the focus of the study being 'spiritual life'. This resulted in an initial caution about the concept of the study, the need for it or what might be asked. No one was put under pressure to take part; but once people started to talk, they became more willing to share ideas, and in some cases others asked to be included in the interviews, even though they had originally declined.

Although the nature of the study had been made clear in advance, some participants remained concerned that the conversation would be about faith. At the end of one visit, the manager said: 'It's entirely different from what I thought it was going to be. I thought it would be more of a religious discussion.' During another visit a volunteer said with apparent relief: 'This isn't really about religion, it's just about wellbeing.'

Managing expectations about outcomes of listening can also be a challenge, the nature of which depends on how the encounter has been presented. Most managers of homes, and some volunteers, wanted to provide information that could influence future policy or practice: they would explain how a change in some practical area such as the speed with which simple repairs to the decoration or fabric of the building happened, could significantly influence the way residents felt about living there. There was a clear expectation that their words would be noted and would result in an improved procedure.

Snapshot: Just a small thing

The dining room was brilliantly sunny, the flowers on each table bringing the summer inside. I did feel a little guilty about the biscuit crumbs on the clean white tablecloth, and surreptitiously manoeuvred them under the saucer, even while knowing that really the housekeeper Marian would not judge me. I asked Marian, as I always did towards the end of a visit, what her one wish for the home would be if she could wave a magic wand over it. 'Blinds for these windows,' she said with little hesitation. 'It gets too hot in here sometimes, but I don't want to draw the curtains and shut out the view, I just want to pull a blind down a bit.' It did seem quite a small thing, for a whole magic wish, but I nodded. 'It does seem such a small thing,' she laughed, 'but it means a lot to the people who eat here every day'.

Elderly residents, however, more often indicated that they wanted to be heard because it was a way of sharing their lives, their feelings and their experiences. A notable exception to this general observation was when the subject of security was raised; for example, people who had lost overnight residential care really wanted the message that this distressed them to be acted upon. This theme will be considered later, when the key factors in creating a home are explored.

The perceived purpose of the encounter influences the nature of what people will raise and discuss. Had the study been directive, with a series of specific questions aimed at ascertaining satisfaction levels with, for example, catering, personal care or physical comfort, such questions would almost certainly be answered with an affirmative, negative or a grading on a scale. This would feed directly into an assessment of the home, and is a valid approach to reporting. However, it does not permit the type of interaction that recognises the respondent as an individual, enabling them to choose what and how to share, so it remains limited, valuing only the information but not the person.

CHAPTER 4

WHAT MAKES A HOME?
Relationships of Spiritual Care

Finding a family

The study undertaken for The Abbeyfield Society centred on their homes rather than care in the community: Abbeyfield has 570 housing schemes and residential care homes in the UK, with 2,000 staff and 4,500 volunteers, accommodating 7,000 residents (8,000 worldwide).

While objectives were set in terms of exploring and improving lives, there were no preconceptions or assumptions, as the purpose was to listen to voices and interpret these sensitively into guidance for the conduct of the charity. In the event, there were naturally some surprises, not least how profound the implications of the study are for the future of elderly care.

Spending time in homes with older people as part of a research project is not just about listening; it is also about absorbing, and being absorbed. About being part of those lives, partially and temporarily, but nevertheless travelling beyond observation into feeling. I hope that by sharing the feelings as well as the observations, this chapter will reveal truths about life lived in a home, and its potential to be transformative when it provides a refuge from loneliness and neglect, and feeds physical and spiritual hunger. These truths hold profound implications for individuals and society and also hold the answers to practical questions of how to provide more while reducing the overall financial costs to society.

The central paradigm is family life. Many older people are alone in their 'family homes', and have no family nearby, or certainly not present much of the day. Current wisdom is that we must strive to help people stay in the house where they may have brought up their family, to which they have deep emotional attachment, and where they have friends and neighbours. But this conventional 'wisdom' ignores the changes that will have taken place to the person and the house as time goes by: the house is no longer a place where other people are in the room next door; it may feel isolated and insecure, with strange noises heard or imagined at night. It presents barriers in the form of stairs, heavy furniture, doors that need to be locked, vital items that mysteriously move from their accustomed places. The person has also changed and is perhaps no longer mobile enough to reach into cupboards, to go out shopping or hop on a bus to see friends. The burden of living grows, but the desire to cling on to the known can remain strong.

This research suggests that it is not the house that is important to feeling secure and nurtured, but the community. People can rebuild family life in a new home, if it is a community where they feel rooted, their isolation is addressed, and their critical needs met. The important factors are primarily: a safe environment that fosters good relationships, recognition and being valued as an individual; enjoyable nourishing food; and personal care relevant to the individual's needs. Such simple things are arguably human rights, not complicated to envisage yet apparently challenging to provide.

The argument evidenced by the Abbeyfield surveys is that the challenges are surmountable and more than that, the financial and societal savings in providing what really matters to older people, as opposed to what other people think they want, are potentially life changing for us all as a society.

This chapter now attempts to reveal that evidence by looking in detail at the constellation of factors that nurture relationships, and how they need to work together to be effective in creating a favourable environment for wellbeing.

Snapshot: Sun and shade

Another hot day in Essex, this time in an old market town. I arrive quite early at the house and the manager takes me into a small courtyard, overhung with trailing plants and sunshades, the doors of the residents' studio rooms opening onto it. Three or four people are eating a cooked breakfast at wooden patio tables. George is in a wheelchair, and Jane brings him a tray with eggs and bacon, toast and tea. She helps him position it comfortably, and pauses for a word, to check all is well and agree it is indeed a lovely morning. I sip my own tea, and ask George how long he has been a resident, trying not to impede his eating with anything demanding of lengthy answers.

Later I talk to Jane. She looks over to George, the tray has gone, the tea and an unopened newspaper remain. She turns to me: 'When they thank me, I say to them, you've done your bit in life, now it's your turn to be looked after.'

Safely home again

We often talk in terms of the flesh and the spirit, but it is not be possible to consider nurturing the latter without awareness of its interaction with the former: it is very clear that the physical environment affects people's sense of self, which in turn affects all aspects of wellbeing.

The question of security in a home is an excellent example of this interaction. Nearly all residents and staff cite this as an issue that is absolutely vital to peace of mind, and when asked what mattered most to residents' sense of wellbeing, one Chair of Trustees said, 'Security, companionship, good food – but of the three, when it comes down to it, security.'

Security is mainly associated with the presence of other people, both during the day and at night. This presence of others is likely to be one of the factors most lacking when older people stay on in their family home with intermittent care during the day. One who had recently moved compared the discontinuity of care in her own home, when she was dependent on different people coming in for short periods, with the situation in her new home; asked if life was better in the latter she treated the question as hardly necessary: 'Of course it is!'

Security is both a practical and an emotional issue: if a resident is anxious in the night, they want to hear a familiar voice, either on the phone or in person. They much prefer the presence of someone overnight, and while this is the norm in nursing homes, it has ceased to be possible in much residential or supported housing. In the absence of this there needs to be confidence in the alarm system.

Feelings of safety are associated with long-term, settled relationships and the knowledge that there is someone there for them who has noticed how they feel. A sense of real security grows with time, as residents learn to build trust in staff, and is essential to an environment in which people can flourish.

Another critical factor in creating a home is the way in which food is prepared and served. People living in residential care are alert to and appreciate the quality of the food, tables being nicely laid, a dedicated space for meals, personal service and most importantly shared meals providing a routine to the day. One lady said it was the single thing which had most transformed her life, 'being able to eat delicious things', and another, 'I love joining in with the meals.' The impact on overall health of nutritious balanced food, in the form of regular hot meals as opposed to snacks, cannot be overemphasised. Staff and relatives observed changes in older people in terms of physical strength, mobility and mental health that they ascribed without hesitation to this factor.

There are significant benefits when meals are taken together at least once a day. Not only is appetite stimulated by company, but also as one person said, 'We sit down together, and it makes us like a family again.' As well as fostering a family atmosphere and encouraging conversation, mealtimes represent an opportunity for managers and staff to unobtrusively monitor wellbeing and address risk of isolation. In fact, shared meals have such an impact that volunteers and managers who had experienced homes where there were additional shared meals felt that one meal a day together was not sufficient. Residents also liked afternoon teas and coffee mornings, not just for company, but again to provide structure in the day. The arrangement does have the risk of any tension or conflict at the table deterring people from eating and staff need to keep a close eye on this, but residents can also be sensitive to maintaining a harmonious atmosphere.

Snapshot: The Goldilocks factor

'The porridge here is perfect.' Martha puts down her magazine to give me her full attention. 'No one ever made it like I made it for myself until I came here, and I do like a wee bit of porridge for breakfast.'

'What are the lunches like?'

'Everything's good, they make meat and potatoes and so on, and a very nice pudding. But to be honest, I'd be happy with some porridge.' I ask about supper and wait – is the answer inevitable? 'They're lovely people, the cook makes a nice supper, but sometimes I say, thanks, Jeannie, but I'll just have a wee bit of your porridge.'

One of the most important factors in the enjoyment of food and the resulting improved health are the cooks: when they are engaged in the life of the home, understand individual needs and enjoy their role (as one said, 'I love this job!') their impact is profound. Residents will relate to the cook as being part of the family; kitchens may be out of bounds, but kitchen doors can be open to allow the tempting smell of baking to emerge, and conversation largely not inhibited by the threshold.

As with meals, so with gardens. They can play a range of roles in the life of a home: encourage mobility and exercise; provide a connection to nature; offer an extra 'room' and lift the spirits. Gardens that are laid out with thought – offering, for example, summerhouses, statues, water features, easy-to-follow paths, raised flowerbeds and fruit trees – can be used as extensions of the communal space, provide quiet areas and in good weather make teas and breakfasts more attractive.

Many older people express an interest in watching birds, and like to have nest boxes in the garden; for those unable to go out, a webcam in the nest, transmitted to a screen in a quiet communal area, would be a benefit.

Views from residents' windows over the garden, and from the gardens into the landscape beyond, are not only uplifting, but where many of the residents come from a rural background this helps to keep a connectedness to community and past life. 'Garden rooms' can also create a bridge with the outside world, and are one of the features that most residents and staff want if it is not already present.

During my research a manager told me that the garden was 'of great emotional significance' to the residents. This was sometimes, but not necessarily, the result of working in it: some people found joy in gardening, but others did not welcome any expectation that they would be involved in the job.

The importance of décor that ensures an individual, warm and welcoming atmosphere is crucial in fostering good relationships. The home must indeed be a home: residents, visitors and staff want to feel at ease, they are not seeking an anonymous hotel or a hospital. Homes that have residents' paintings, photos and books in communal areas, as well as in individual rooms, become shared spaces, where everyone is included and known. The potential problem is that those choosing a home for a loved one may be attracted by the styling that they would expect from a hotel, where the same theme and muted luxury is replicated in every room. It is important to listen to older people in this respect: I found that residents are keen to talk about the individuality of their rooms, and seem to prefer houses where each room has a distinctive shape, outlook and positioning; as one said, 'Each room is different, so it's a personal place.'

One of the most valued communal assets is a 'real' fire in a fireplace, lit in winter or full of flowers in summer, around which people can gather and reminisce. Another is a piano, both for residents who can play, and for visiting musicians; the piano should be located such that people can gather around it.

Not surprisingly, cleanliness and freshness of all the rooms are vital, not only for health reasons but also to support the dignity and self-respect of everyone. Similarly, good maintenance is important, and it is much better for a home to employ a local part-time person for this purpose rather than to rely on a large contractor who may not be immediately available. The local person becomes known and welcomed and people have more personal control over their lives by being able to ask for help in, for instance, having their personal pictures hung, or a radiator sorted quickly. The arrangement has the added benefit of saving money on contractor costs.

Personal hygiene is a factor that plays a multiple role. Not only do people feel uplifted when their appearance is taken care of and they have clean clothes every day, the interaction between the carer and resident occurs during the process, and both aspects contribute to better family bonds.

Snapshot: Losing life's burdens

The housekeeper points out a well-groomed resident, sitting talking to others in the cosy lounge. 'His wife died, and he was sitting in his kitchen with one chair and a table, and he wasn't eating. Len was just drinking, not going to church, or doing anything. Then he came to us, and he said, "You just took it all away, I don't have to worry about anything." He came here, and he stayed, and he never went back to his old house. He's a new man.'

Given the importance of hygiene, it would be easy to leap to the conclusion that animals would be an unsuitable addition to the environment, but of course that conclusion is illogical insofar as pets fit into many family homes without causing illness; indeed, there are numerous studies that indicate both physical and mental health are improved by companion animals. For many people, having a pet is a source of comfort, love and good memories, and it can be very important to their emotional wellbeing.

There is no reason to forbid pets in sheltered housing, and residential homes can have a 'communal' companion such as a cat. Dogs brought in by staff or family visitors provide great enjoyment, and nearly all residents whom I interviewed put contact with companion animals near the top of their wish list. One manager said that the only time she was told off by a resident was when she forgot to take in her dog!

The creation or appreciation of art and music have a strong spiritual dimension. Residents not only enjoy listening to music, from classical performers to 'sing-alongs', it is also the case that singing is an effective way of bringing people together, supporting an emotional bond and hence relationships. Traditional arts and crafts are also effective in this respect, and if classes cannot be brought into the home, the University of the Third Age represents a good resource in helping some residents take up (or share) new interests. Resources from the local community can also be drawn upon, and help maintain a connection with it: for example, the local museum curator may be invited to visit, both to bring artefacts and to collect stories.

However, it is important to recognise that some older people are equally happy just sitting watching others, and for many, simply talking can be as fulfilling and welcome as any organised activity.

Another type of activity that plays a role in emotional wellbeing is the outing, because it acts as important 'milestone' in communal life, being something to plan and look forward to. Arranging and running outings is not without problems: the need for toilet visits (cited as a 'very prominent' issue and one that deterred people from participation), issues of frailty, mobility and access, and the requirement for a reliable minibus.

All these are barriers, but can be overcome in a number of ways, such as having plenty of volunteers to help. It is also best to avoid the 'unknown'; people like going back to the same places, because they 'can picture it' and feel reassured. Venues or events that have been designed to cope with mobility problems also reduce anxiety; for example, using a canal boat adapted for disability.

There is a spiritual dimension to this issue, insofar as people feel in some way diminished when the possibility of getting out and of interaction with the outside world is reduced.

The family paradigm

The observations above, concerned primarily with the 'shared living' environment of the home or supported accommodation, all have relevance to the formation of relationships. I have suggested that the 'right' relationships are critical to all aspects of optimising the lives of older people living together, but what is 'right'? What do these relationships look like in practical terms, how do they impact on emotional and spiritual as well as physical health and are they achievable?

Caring in this context (and it is important to note that staff and residents more often use the word 'love' when describing it) appears not to be consciously transactional, but more about feeling and responding. A manager articulated it thus: 'Care is about everyone's social and spiritual needs...staff must take a holistic rather than care-oriented approach.' This goes beyond any notion of duty, and the role of the employers is to provide support and training directed towards fostering this attitude, so that caring can be expressed effectively, rather than letting something so spiritually important become part of a brave new world of care plans and tick boxes.

Nearly everyone whom I met used the concept of 'family' as a main reference point when describing their feelings about their home: for example, they spoke of 'family bonds', 'We are a family, and we support each other', and relationships with each other that 'they would never have had on their own, so it's like another family'.

It is clear this is a critical factor in promoting spiritual wellbeing and that it is possible to create institutions that are not 'institutionalised'. Managers who are aware of this actively aim to promote it by keeping matters such as health and safety issues and paperwork 'in the background' so that they do not interfere with the family dynamics. The relationships in these families are referred to in various ways; in some cases, managers are seen in the role of a 'mother', but others would see themselves as a daughter 'with ten mothers to care for'.

No family can be happy all the time, and discord will occur; if relationships were to break down anxiety or alienation could be the result, and the family paradigm demands vigilance from staff, who must be prepared to mediate, and to represent the best points of each person to the other, to promote harmony.

Snapshot: There's difficult and difficult...

'What do we do about difficult people?' muses Gail. 'Well, sometimes you can't really do much. Mostly people do fit in, but I remember Maggie, she was a terror. We had a dozen people here then, just two of them men, and Maggie wanted them to herself. Any new lady arriving got accused of trying to get her hands on them! It wasn't funny; she took to driving her mobility scooter around, trying to knock people down.'

'So what did you do?'

'As it happened, she decided she wanted to leave anyway, so that was that. But I do wonder what might have happened otherwise.'

As will already be evident from the preceding observations, one of the most notable findings of the research is the critical role of the manager in setting the tone of communal life, and a number of respondents described them as the 'hub' of the home, or even as its 'soul': 'The manager knows everything and understands everything', as a member of staff said. Residents refer to their managers as listener, mediator and a source of comfort and information. This implies that there is a potential risk to the wellbeing of the home when this 'hub' person leaves. This may not be a frequent occurrence; in Abbeyfield for example, and probably in similar charities, managers stayed an average of nine years, and those I met said they would be reluctant to retire until a satisfactory replacement was found.

The impact can be ameliorated in a number of ways. Other staff and volunteers or trustees can provide continuity and involve residents in appointment decisions. In fact, when the move does happen, residents can cope very well if good structures are in place and there is a strong community spirit. As one resident said, 'They all improve. They're strange when they start.'

The real problems were identified with adapting to constant change, such as the introduction of relief staff, rather than one major change for which everyone could be prepared, and which was carefully handled.

While managers contribute to the life of the home in part by ensuring a safe environment free of practical worries, one of their main roles is to be a listener, and they must give priority to this function even if it means dealing with other matters in their own time. Putting in substantial time is rarely grudged, indeed managers find it hard to distance themselves from the home when not on duty, perhaps because it is so much a 'family'. When this matter is discussed, the response is that they gain enjoyment themselves from the interactions, it need not all be serious and intense but can be joyful. Sometimes the manager's family also becomes part of the extended 'family', with husbands and children regular visitors and often helpers.

These relationships can be sustained over distance; for example, staff or managers may visit any residents in hospital, sometimes frequently, because they see that as the natural way for a family member to behave, and because other residents would be seeking a report.

In terms of attitudes, relationships and roles, staff can respond and act similarly to managers in creating 'family' when they are committed to the caring role, have close relationships with residents and see themselves as part of a team drawing support mainly from their colleagues. These factors make them part of the 'family', giving to it and in turn being nurtured not only by managers and peers, but also by residents. This essential aspect of reciprocity will be addressed much more fully later.

Creating and sustaining bonds

Again, it is critical to the wellbeing of all concerned that there are established relationships of trust, allowing anything that is amiss to be noticed: 'Staff tune in to each other's needs', as one explained. A network of relationships demands flexibility, and whilst staff may be employed to undertake a certain role, this dynamic means that they view themselves primarily as part of a group enterprise. This means, for instance that cooks might also go on outings, cleaners talk and listen as they work, managers both serve and partake of meals.

Consequently, there can be a high level of alertness to need and the possibility of responding quickly within the daily routine. An excellent example of this model of natural communication was described to me:

> Sometimes she [the cleaner] gets stuck in a room for a long time, which is a good thing, because they're chatting, so she gets feedback, and she'll say [to the manager], what's wrong with so-and-so today, she seems a bit down. So cleaning goes out of the window, but you've supported someone.

A close community cannot be achieved without forming bonds of affection, and this means that managers and staff may feel the loss quite considerably when a resident dies. Their coping mechanism is to try to move on with an awareness that other residents also need them, and to cultivate an attitude of acceptance based on the inevitability given the advanced age of many in their care. Residents are aware how badly affected by a death managers can be, and express concern for them such that each can comfort the other.

Listening is critical to supportive relationships, but it takes time, and the family dynamic can only flourish if schedules enable it to. This can be achieved in part through the type of multi-tasking described above, but there may also need to be a conscious decision to pause and listen regardless of other tasks. Volunteers are important in this context, not only to provide a listening ear themselves, but also to take over administrative tasks to create a greater pool of time. Managers often cite the motto 'People over Paperwork' in this context.

Those employed as carers in turn feel nurtured by the relationships, and speak of them being 'emotionally enriching'. They also observe that residents feel more at peace when they see staff interaction is harmonious, and that any dispute between staff has a damaging effect on residents.

Where homes are fortunate enough to have them, volunteers also play a critical role as part of the 'family', offering additional listening time from a different standpoint, which works most effectively if they can come in with reasonable frequency and consistency such that relationships of understanding can form. Male volunteers may have a particular role, when there are things that male residents prefer to discuss with other men, and when staff are predominantly female.

Some volunteers also enjoy doing organisational work that releases employees' time for more personal interaction; the role can be varied, and need not demand frequent attendance. For example, they can pick up prescriptions, help organise events, help on outings (which may need one-to-one assistance) or teach their skills, on everything from IT to building birdboxes. Another role for volunteers is to 'look out for' people and observe from a more independent stance what is happening so that any problems can be quickly addressed.

When either staff or residents leave, the family is to an extent 'broken' and has to re-form. On numerous occasions, I was told that when staff leave, they maintain relationships with residents and colleagues by 'popping back in' to chat or for a special occasion, and by still helping with events. They rarely disappear completely. As people leave and join the family, the character of the home changes over time, and is particularly influenced by the personality of the manager.

The size of the home also affects the way bonds form. In larger ones, there is a greater diversity of people, and therefore more opportunity to find others where friendships will naturally happen, so groups develop, although the wise manager takes steps to ensure these do not become cliques. Also, with more staff, supportive relationships grow with cleaners and other carers, rather than necessarily all being with the manager.

In smaller homes, closeness demands more tolerance, but also fosters greater knowledge of one another. One manager said she thought that this meant sensitivity to one another was nurtured, contributing to spiritual fulfilment.

There is a difference in terms of listening opportunities between larger and smaller homes: in the former, there is less of the informal contact time that happens within a small, close knit group, so there may be a need for more formal times to be set aside, over coffee mornings, afternoon teas and so on.

Although relationships within the 'new family', formed through listening and sharing meals, are such a critical feature of the nurturing residential home, for most people (but there are exceptions) seeing and keeping in contact with friends and family remains a very important part of life. If someone is already part of the locality, this is normally easier to achieve, as residents may have close links to people living in the town, be part of clubs or a church there and meet old friends when they go to the local shops.

Snapshot: Christmas in Northern Ireland

We are seated round the dining table, substantial in every sense: the hot food is served; there are maybe ten residents there together. Some are quite quiet, others want to talk. Beyond the picture window is the compact, cobbled town square, and we are watching workmen put up the Christmas tree. The square is busy with shoppers hunched against the cold, the retail options ranging from the universal and expected, to those that looked as though they may have been embedded here for a hundred years or more, steadily growing a loyal clientele. Some of the people around the table explain how they used to go into those shops on errands as

> children, to pick up the bread or meat, and maybe even buy some sweets. They know and are known.
>
> 'They're putting up the tree early because you're visiting us,' jokes Margaret, sitting next to me. Two people along is Agnes; she tells me she was the town recorder here during her working days. 'There's nothing she doesn't know about everyone out there,' says Margaret.

However, there should be encouragement to ensure that links are maintained, and visitors must be welcomed as they would have been to the person's previous home. Managers and staff have to manage this delicate balance, such that jealousy between those with and without visitors is minimised and other residents do not feel invaded, and in part this can be achieved through the physical environment. It is important that families of different residents are helped to feel comfortable with one another.

Providing an environment for family conversation can be difficult if there is just one large, communal room – it is important to have a variety of smaller common rooms, preferably with a facility to make hot drinks. The right environment will stimulate conversation through artwork or artefacts, quiet places to sit, shared meals at weekends. An overnight guest room is ideal for visitors who are too distant to drop in, and a table tennis table keeps children occupied, possibly in taking on their grandparents.

The family in the community

If homes are made welcoming to 'blood' family and friends, contact with residents is facilitated and visitors are not 'just sitting'. For example, they can join coffee mornings, help with outings and special events, play the piano or share a hobby, so becoming part of the 'new family'. When this happens, then even after the death of a resident, staff report that they will continue to support and grieve with relatives and be supported by them.

Staff can facilitate residents going out with families, by reminding them of the time, helping them dress suitably, and so on. Where families are physically remote, they can also help with communication, phoning, writing letters or setting up Skype.

Not every resident wants contact with all their family, and this needs to be respected. For some, loss of family may be upsetting; for others it may be liberating. In some cases there may have been, or still be, difficulties and managers need to act as mediators or find others who can. The relationship between families and staff is another aspect of the complex support network that exists.

A further factor to be taken into consideration is the wider community and locality. In some homes and sheltered accommodation, the majority of the residents will have lived in the locality most of their lives. In others, many have come to the area to be near relatives. In all homes, there will be some mix of the two.

The extent of the 'feeder' areas – and some may be much wider than others – affects the relationship with the local community. A home with strong links into its community may well be able to create an internal environment that reflects the environment from which its residents are drawn – for example, one Chair said that the people of the town had a strong independent streak, and this had to be respected in the incoming residents.

Smaller homes in small towns and more rural areas are likely to have more residents from the close vicinity, and this results in their being taken out by or going to visit friends as well as family. It also means they are known when out and about, not just as a resident but as a person who had a role in the community, which helps to maintain a sense of self.

This is a two-way issue, and a more 'porous' boundary between home and community is beneficial. If managers make an effort to reach out – for example, by inviting elderly people in the locality to come in at Christmas or holding 'open house' with refreshments – this will play a role in involving residents in their wider community, as they may well want to be with people of all ages. It will also enable the community to benefit, by not losing the experience and voices of its most elderly members.

These observations underline the importance to spiritual health of certain critical factors: the home should be part of its local community; staff need to be in post long term, in order to build relationships, be willing to give priority to listening, and act as teams so that work can be handed around to free up listening time at critical moments. These issues are addressed further when we look at the concept of 'mutual chaplaincy'.

A sense of self and meaning in life

Families may have their pros and cons, but the family model for older people in care offers a way of providing mutual listening and opportunities to contribute to communal living that are critical to reflection; to feeling known and understood as an individual being; and to gaining a sense that life has had, and does have meaning.

As Kirkegaard stated, 'Life can only be understood backwards, but it must be lived forwards' (Collins 1953). The vital importance of a 'life narrative' as providing the difference between integrity and despair is well accepted: a way for people to understand, make sense of and come to terms with all they have done and been and still are.

This is not just a matter of going over old memories, although memory is an important factor; it is also about being listened to, putting one's own life narrative in a wider spiritual context and dealing with unresolved issues if possible. It also means accepting negatives as well as positives about the past. Hilary Cottam of the think tank 'Participle' made the point (Radio 4, Today programme, 18.12.13) that when elderly people are lonely, they tend to go over bad memories and forget good ones, whereas when talking to others in relationships of trust, they will spend more time on good memories.

Capturing memories can have an advantage over and above contributing directly to life stories, in that such memories can be useful after the onset of dementia, for example to ensure someone can wear their favourite colour or be offered their special cake.

To ensure active and useful listening, a range of informal, personal opportunities needs to become part of the everyday routine, creating the right atmosphere to avoid the process feeling invasive: managers speak of being 'enablers' and taking the conversation in the right direction to give opportunities rather than forcing the pace. There can be many triggers for sharing memories: personal photo collections, photo-based games and quizzes, collages, sing-alongs, reminiscence groups or themed events such St George's Day. In one case a local poet visited to collect stories, and returned with a video recording them. But an equally important time for sharing is during routines of personal care such as dressing, or during room cleaning.

When staff talk about incidents from their own lives, for example a daughter's wedding, this is a good opening for memories, and enables natural, relational sharing rather than a formalised process.

Snapshot: Never mind the television

A volunteer relates a short but telling story: 'I used to run the film show… One afternoon I went round and the television set wouldn't work. I was playing with the television set, trying to make it work… I was sitting on the floor by the television and stayed there for the next three-quarters of an hour just chatting. At the end I said, "Sorry about that, I'm very sorry about the film show," and one lady said, "Doesn't matter, we've enjoyed sitting here and having a good blather".'

Most interestingly, during my research I found that many people said or implied that this sharing can only happen when trust and relationships have developed. They used phrases such as: 'You have to know people well' and 'It's not like in six months they'll build up the trust, the older generation are very private'. This suggests that formal counselling may be less effective in helping build a life narrative, and facilitating shared time within the 'family' may be more so. Knitting clubs, coffee mornings and meal times all engender listening and sharing.

Listening may be one to one or a group process: 'Every time we sit down to tea, it's about listening' as one person said. Some residents wish to share memories with one another, some just with staff; some residents listen to others, some just want to talk. Managers must act as mediators at times, to ensure everyone is heard.

There is generally recognition by the staff that not all listening and memories will be pleasant. In one home, a resident had memories of an attack she had suffered when younger, and another of previous alcoholism. Both wanted to talk to staff and some other residents about this, but at the right time for them.

Listeners may be able to help by showing acceptance: 'I can't make it change, but I can say, "I understand, I really do"', said a member of staff. Such challenging aspects of residents' life stories are quite rare, and one manager suggested that this could be due to an earlier acceptance or resolution: 'I think they've come to terms with it long before...I think they've dealt with a lot of things.'

There is also recognition that people need to feel validated and whole; when I asked about what helped people to feel at peace with life, both residents and staff talked about growing to feel comfortable with they had done and achieved, and who they were.

An important aspect of life narrative with older people is not to interact with them as though this were a story that had already ended and needed neatly tidying up – there should not be an unspoken assumption that they are close to death. On the contrary, life narratives are continuing, so people spoke of sharing joint memories created since their arrival: of amusing incidents, past residents and so on. Similarly, there should not be an assumption that older people only wish to look back; several of the residents I spoke with had a wide variety of current interests, from family to environmental issues.

Yet death is naturally ever present in a place where elderly people are living together, and family bonds can help in living with this reality: 'We cope because we're a big, family caring group,' said one volunteer, explaining why it is easier to talk to one another about bereavement rather than an external counsellor. Sharing memories of the deceased was important and this comfort could only be found with others who knew the resident themselves.

Sharing life stories is not only valuable to the person speaking, who is articulating aspects of their life's meaning, but also to the listener, who reaps the harvest with them. Residents may want to listen as well as talk, and participate in other people's life stories such as the births, marriages and illnesses that affect other residents or the staff they care about.

Finding meaning in life comes in part from being reconciled to the past, but it also flows from contributing in the present, as both bring a sense of wholeness. It is clear when observing the life of residential homes that nurture spiritual health, that residents often 'look out' for each other in a great variety of ways, and that as a result they feel both useful and valued as individuals. It is also critical for some residents to seek and find opportunities to contribute to family life in practical ways; for example, by laying the table nicely, or seeing their artwork on the walls.

This has to be treated sensitively; there must be no expectation of residents taking on jobs, and in one situation where they believed they had been tasked with the upkeep of a garden there was considerable resentment. Some residents actively wish to help each other, and find ways of doing so, while some will have difficulty in giving or receiving, and may even feel patronised. There are those, although a minority, who find the 'family' model unpalatable, but are willing to tolerate each other even when they are not naturally compatible, and get along as 'neighbours'.

The nature of 'independence' for older people

When someone moves into a sheltered house or care home, their lives will inevitably undergo considerable change. Different residents take different approaches: some bring as many of their possessions and furnishings as possible, others buy everything afresh, seeing this as a new phase of life. As one resident said to me (very positively): 'I walked out of the house and never looked back; I have had to make a new life for myself.'

Critical observations from the Abbeyfield research call into question the whole edifice of belief about the nature and meaning of 'independence' for older people. Community care plans, the concerns of friends and family and the need to protect the home as an inheritance are all based on the assumption that older people are happier and more secure if they can be helped to stay in their own house as long as possible. Older people themselves nearly always assume this is the ideal as well, when the truth is that their determination to retain 'independence' can become a daily struggle for survival and dignity.

Snapshot: Just in time

The small garden outside the lattice window is being prepared for the annual Strawberry Tea that brings together residents, friends and local people, some of them long-time supporters. We are in a summerhouse, though it's also a winter house, with heating and a coffee-maker. Keith, Chair

> of the Home's Trustees, is watching an elderly lady putting out tablecloths. We are talking about death and dying, and he is very matter-of-fact: people move in at a later and later age, holding on in their own homes until they cannot manage any longer, and then time runs out for them. 'They used to get 10 or 15 years here, get settled, now we are used to them dying quite soon.' He indicates the lady with her gingham tablecloths. 'Sometimes it works out. She was no more than a vegetable when she arrived. Wrong medication, it turned out. Now she's the liveliest person here.'

Reliance on short intermittent visits and the delivery of assistance such as grocery orders can slide into the nightmare of being put to bed early in the evening with no option for toileting other than adult nappies, no way of safely accessing a cup of hot tea, being subject to fears about intruders and prey to depression and loneliness. Given that not all residential care is perfect, that it conjures up the image (and sometimes the reality) of people sitting around the walls of a room staring into space or watching television, and that news stories focus on mistreatment and exploitation, it is nevertheless surprising how often elderly people still equate moving into care with 'the workhouse'. The Victorian workhouses were finally abolished by Act of Parliament in 1930, although they continued as Public Assistance Institutions beyond that date, but their shadow still seems to linger in the collective memory.

Yet the spectre apparently most feared by older people, based on the testimony of staff, is isolation. Almost without exception, residents said one of the greatest benefits of moving into care was 'company' and 'friendliness'. One said, 'When you're isolated it's not good. Just having the company is wonderful. It's an enormous difference.' In stark contrast, findings by Age UK (May 2014), note the increasing social isolation of elderly people living at home, many of whom consider their pet or the television to be their most important form of company.

However, residents have often left their home of many years and may equally fear loss of privacy. Both potential problems threaten peace of mind and human flourishing, and there is a vital balance to be struck in this respect. When the move is made, feelings of loss can be ameliorated by their new 'family' getting to know and really understand them. The new arrival is reassured and not struggling to be an individual again.

This question of maintaining the right balance between community or 'family' and personal individuality and sense of self is critical to spiritual and emotional wellbeing, and managers and staff must be aware of this; one said it was important that people had their own voice, and felt in control of their lives: 'I think it's very important that the person is still their own person.' The role of the manager is to help without being obtrusive, so that residents feel they are able to control their lives. Similarly, they must be facilitated in finding the balance between interdependence and self-articulation.

One way of enabling this is to recognise people's past and experience by making available small jobs that allow them to feel valued. One manager, when asked what helped people to feel more content, said: 'I think if they're able to do something, to help one another... It's their home, but they have to be part of the home as well.' She spoke of a lady who liked to clear the table, and a man who did the weeding in the summer; these apparently minor matters are important in nurturing a sense of self after a period of transition.

Older people, in common with everyone, need to nurture their individuality in relation to others, without being totally absorbed into a communal life, such that living alone in a room or flat does not equate to loneliness, and there is freedom of choice as to the level of company at any one time. It is important to personal integrity that residents are not 'hounded' into companionship. As one manager said: 'There's this big family, but they don't like to be disturbed once they're behind their doors.' Offers of support should not be intrusive or interfere with the 'real' family relationships that a good home will make sure remain cultivated.

Privacy can be maintained if there are clear (albeit unwritten) 'rules' about visiting that are adopted by communal consent and may vary as the composition of the home changes. For example, in some homes this may only be by invitation, in others, visitors knock on doors before entering, and must not knock too early in the morning. When these unwritten rules are broken, it can cause problems, and the manager may need to intervene. Most homes develop their own 'norm', although this is easier to achieve in smaller establishments. Accepted practice comes into play, and it is important not to disturb a tradition that people have got used to, for example, if there is a change of management.

The use of communal spaces is another factor in finding the privacy/interdependence balance. It is essential that some rooms are not earmarked as dining or television, but are more intimate and favour conversation; if there is too little communal space, for example the dining room and lounge are combined, this inhibits conversation.

Boundaries about physical contact are also a consideration: managers and staff need to be aware of who welcomes comfort and cuddles and who does not, and this will change as mutual relationships of trust develop. Similarly, there are boundaries with sharing memories, which will not be comfortable for all, and where privacy must be respected.

Snapshot: Loners aren't lonely

'I'm a bit of a loner,' muses Keith, sitting in a garden room in a Kent care home, with a book and cup of tea. 'But when you do want to be with people, in the front room we can read papers and have a chat to one another and at lunch time, of course, we have a meal together, and there's plenty of time to talk to your friends. I'm not a great talker, I'm not like Jean downstairs, she can talk for England! Sometimes you see somebody looking really down in the dumps, you can have a chat to them, and often it lifts them, and it lifts you as well.'

A balance that appears to be delicate will in fact work quite well as long as the residents know what is acceptable and are able to live with it, but problems can arise if residents are in the 'wrong' home, or are unable to understand due to conditions such as dementia (this is explored in Chapter 6).

Mealtimes also provide an important aspect of balance, preventing isolation but limiting contact to a known time and place; a matter that one volunteer recognised when she said: 'They all come together, and then they go apart. Going apart to their rooms probably helps them to stay good friends.'

The importance of communal mealtimes in encouraging family bonds and ensuring good nutrition has already been addressed. But it must be acknowledged that the potential downside of this arrangement is that people have little control over choice of food or time of eating, which could erode independence and sense of self.

However, this may be another myth ripe to be challenged. My findings are surprising, as to how little this apparent loss of independence worried most residents: what they were really interested in was the quality, freshness and home cooking. In fact, some residents would actively prefer not to control the menu. One said that surprise was part of the fun of meals – 'We like to wonder what's for tea' – and another said it was less stressful not to have the bother of choosing.

This issue of choice can in any case be partially ameliorated, if managers are conscious of it as a potential problem and take the right steps. For example, independent flats in sheltered housing will have kitchenettes and residential homes can have 'pods' and 'galleys' for preparation of snacks, or coffee stations (some in delightfully unexpected places such as the garden house). Again, the cook or housekeeper has a major role to play by meeting requests for special cakes, making sure that people choose the menu on their birthdays, and taking on board feedback through meetings and 'like/dislike' sheets.

Most people moving into a home have the common sense and resilience to recognise that there will be sacrifices of choice, and can accept this with equanimity; as one said, 'There is a variety of ages, and some people are quite frail, so it would be difficult to offer food choices.' However, management must in turn take all matters to do with food and mealtimes seriously, as these issues affect all aspects of wellbeing.

Given that, as one resident said, 'the kitchen is the hub of a home', there is also an element of sacrifice in losing access to the place of food creation. In some homes, it is possible to overcome health and safety issues by having a partial division between the kitchen and dining areas such that residents can sit in the area when they want, and have a chance to talk about the food they would like on the menu as well as sampling the baking as it emerges from the oven.

However, if health and safety reasons make the kitchen inaccessible, then the cook needs to spend time chatting with people and sharing the baking in the lounge.

Similarly, residents' experience can be recognised and their sense of independence improved if they are involved in appointing a new manager when change takes place. This process was described by a volunteer in an Abbeyfield home:

> When we were interviewing, [one resident] sat on the panel. Another resident was down in the sunroom and as the applicants came in she showed them upstairs. We had a meeting prior to doing the interviews with the residents asking them what the qualities they would like to see in a new house manager, and the first one was to be a good cook. Also that they listen, in fact [another resident], although she didn't do any of the scoring, after each applicant went out she was able to jot down notes and say what she thought. She thought that [person appointed] would be gentle and that she would listen.

It should be a matter of good practice to involve residents in the selection process as much as possible, not only for their own sake, but also because it is likely to make running the establishment smoother and easier, and identify unsuitable candidates at an earlier stage.

All these factors facilitate true independence, which is not a matter of living alone, but of having one's self-identity and past experience respected, as a person of any age would hope, and should expect. The real problem is that the myth of elderly independence inhibits the move to more suitable and less lonely accommodation for too long, such that it may not be made until much later in life, often after the age of 90. As a result of this, and of what one trustee called 'often chaotic care at home', residents are more frail and less likely to live sufficiently long for enduring communities to be established.

The corollary is that they must then move again, and I was given many examples of how much a second move threatens people's emotional and spiritual wellbeing, from a 'family' environment where they are settled and known, to another establishment: dementia care home, nursing home or hospital. This is hard on the person themselves, and on the other residents, and is wasteful of resources. Reflecting on the consequences of moving again, from one care setting to another, a relative said, 'The day my Mum left Abbeyfield, she started to die...I think when they move, their last little bit of independence has gone.'

Looking at social care through a new lens

It would be foolish to suggest that implementing the good practices indicated by this research would have no financial impact on older people, their families or society. This practical aspect cannot be dismissed by proposing that the happiness and dignity of the older generation is priceless, and is therefore invaluable in monetary terms, although a sense of moral justice may indicate this stance. The fact is that good practice can save scarce resources, and overall optimise the funding that society decides to allocate to caring for its older people.

Residential homes and sheltered housing, run on a non-profit but financially sound basis, have the potential to make the lives of older people and their families less stressful; save costs to the NHS; release relatives who are carers back into employment; free up housing more suitable for young families; and provide other benefits that are analysed in Chapter 5. They have this potential because they can harness the enormous value of recreating 'family' through the concept of mutual chaplaincy that is explored in Chapter 5.

The potential can be unlocked in a number of ways, recognising that good governance and financial management are not inimical to spiritual wellbeing, dignity and autonomy, but underpin them by enabling suitable design of buildings, properly paid and trained staff, a sufficient amount of listening and caring time and good nutritious food. Homes can identify ways of improving their income that are positive, for example by a high level of staff retention, drawing in volunteers from the local community and making sure they are rewarded, and promoting the availability of temporary voids for respite stays.

Money spent on making what should become family homes look like smart hotels to attract relatives is wasted; as one wise manager said: 'The big, posh new homes think they know what elderly people with money want, but really they just want the same as everyone else – a clean warm room, good food, and just someone there for them.'

The 'someone there for them' are their fellow residents, the staff and the manager. Staff training is vital, and honours the time and care that is given, strengthening them in their role and confidence to deal with difficult issues such as bereavement, the onset of dementia and knowing how best to approach residents in emotional difficulty to offer help that is not intrusive. Training, monitoring and rewarding must be seen as valuable in helping the right people do things more effectively, and not as a way of making unsuitable people into good carers: 'It's not teaching them to care, it's supporting them to care.' Several managers I spoke to said that if they could not see evidence of staff loving the residents, they could not keep them indefinitely.

Another way of optimising the value of residential and sheltered housing within and beyond the social care system is to aim for it to be a near-seamless component between leaving one's own home and needing nursing care. Ensuring that residential homes are porous to the local community, with friends easily able to visit and volunteers encouraged, and situating accommodation near a reputable and trusted nursing home or linking different care models on one single site, reduces the fear of the unknown and allows relationships of support to continue.

The role of the Social Services must be part of a society's overall provision, but could be reduced if older people were less reliant on a patchwork of care, emergency situations arose less frequently as a result, and experienced officers' time was used instead in an advisory role, assisting in dealing with other statutory bodies and ensuring the right support at the right time.

Volunteers can be drawn into the home in various ways: I found that many are from families of residents (including deceased residents); some had dropped in from the local community to a cake sale or similar and liked the atmosphere; some younger people had come in under a scheme to teach IT; and in one home speech therapists had come in from their local college and stayed on.

Observations on the financial implications of providing excellence in care based on relational principles should perhaps conclude with a short reflection on commercial provision.

In 2014, 9 per cent of the 9.2million adults over 65 in the UK were receiving some type of social care on a commercial basis (ONS 2016), from large and small (but predominantly small, estimated to be 73% of the total) for-profit and not-for-profit providers. This is not always a sustainable business sector: analysis provided by Moore Stephens' 'Moore Data' service (based on Companies House figures as at 27 July 2017) showed 1,210 financially stressed companies from a total of 7,497 care home companies. One in six care homes was showing signs that it was at risk from a combination of rising employee and agency staff costs, and lack of funding from local authorities. When any service provider to older people fails, or is bought up as an investment, the impact on those in its care is life changing, and can be catastrophic.

Do the analysis and theory proposed in this book indicate that it is impossible for a profit-making company to run a home that meets the criteria for forming family relationships? It would be unjust and untrue to propose that commercial businesses cannot be run in an ethical manner, but that is not the question here. The question is whether sufficient resource can be committed, and justified to shareholders within a plc commercial model, to achieve the levels of staffing, investment in design excellence and building compliance with the guidelines to enable sustainable relationship-centred care. Unless such a commercial model can be made to work, there will always be the risks of either falling below the highest standards, or of failing and closing, both of which are disastrous scenarios for staff and residents alike.

CHAPTER 5

CREATING THE 'HOME FROM HOME'

Whilst the nature of care giving and receiving makes it hard to draw absolute conclusions about what is 'good' or 'bad', it is definitely the case that those involved know whether or not they are content and feel nurtured in their situation, and that the listening observer is able to form sound views as to the extent to which people are thriving. This cannot be a 'tick list' exercise.

For the reasons explored in Chapter 3, the care home or sheltered housing can be seen as a 'relational' home, and the relationships it is capable of supporting provide the critical foundation for wellbeing. Therefore, homes that appear on investigation to work well for all those brought together in them – residents, staff and volunteers – are also very likely to have features in common. Having addressed in the previous chapter how attitudes to care are shaped by perception and expectation, we can now turn to more tangible matters: what are the ingredients of the 'relational home' recipe?

One of the practical issues is the physical environment. Bearing in mind the primary role of realising a 'family' in terms of relationships, the building that nurtures this must reflect the critical features of a family home. Most of us are in the fortunate position of being able to conjure up the vision of a home where we have felt secure, loved and free to grow as an individual.

There may well have been a kitchen which, if it was big enough, became a gathering place not only to share food but also stories, worries, joys, arguments and understanding. A main room of some sort, with treasures everyone had contributed – perhaps drawings from school, holiday mementoes, ornaments, paintings, furniture, all with a history attached. Bedrooms probably reflected the idiosyncrasies of their owners. There was some mess around, which was acceptable if it was 'clean mess', but dirt, especially someone else's grime in the bathroom or kitchen, was unlikely to make you feel settled or comfortable. There might have been pets, or evidence of crafts and games left on tables or floors, or half-read books, or a computer with papers scattered around it.

When you picture your family home, or that of someone you used to enjoy visiting, it is very unlikely that you visualise anything anonymous, perfect or featureless. Nor that you recollect all the people who lived there sitting in silence staring at nothing much. So why should any family home, even if it is one where everyone happens to be elderly, be any different?

Life does not, or should not, end at the door of a care home that is a neatly kept waiting room until death is ready to receive you. There is no need for that and no advantage in it for anyone, so why do we accept it as a norm? It is more than possible for older people to find meaning in life, to feel loved and contented and recognised as individuals. A building can promote or prevent this attainment, by making it easy or difficult to form human bonds.

The use of indoor space

Whether a new build or an existing converted house, the features that make a real home can be recreated in various ways. It is essential that there is more than one communal room, in particular to avoid the scenario of the loud, dominant television. Each common room should have a variety of chairs that are easy to move so that people can sit in reasonable proximity when they wish to talk, or read quietly, or simply enjoy being in a place with other people. Ideally, the main lounge will have a piano and as a focal point, a real or good imitation fire.

If the manager decides that a shared television is desirable, perhaps so that people can discuss what they are watching or choose film shows from a streaming facility, then it should be in a separate room, not the main lounge. Residents should be able to put their own things in the lounge and other communal areas if they wish to: pictures, photos, ornaments, items they would like to explain or show to others and that help their visiting friends and relatives feel welcome.

All these features promote opportunities for conversation, sharing and quiet reflection. One of the most valued communal rooms is the garden room. A conservatory may get too hot or cold, but a brick-built garden room with large windows, greenery and if possible a good view of the garden or landscape beyond encourages exercise in the garden, connects people into their locality and provides plenty of natural light.

Bedrooms should be as individual as possible. This is of course easier in an old, quirky house where each will have different features, but it is perfectly possible to design-in a variety of room shapes, sizes and aspects to new build. Views from windows are also important; many older people benefit mentally from being able to see life going on outside, especially if they can watch children playing or going to school, local shops, a park or even visitors arriving at their home.

The kitchen is at the heart of the home. A good architect will find ways of making the division required for safety purposes as 'permeable' as possible with the dining room, so that the cook can easily talk to residents, and their appetite can be stimulated by the sights and smells of cooking and baking. Similarly, the dining room must be designed and decorated to make the experience of shared meals attractive and encourage pleasurable eating and conversation. One of the features a number of people mentioned as beneficial in the dining room are large windows allowing in as much light as possible, especially during the winter. Again, residents' paintings and other possessions should be accommodated if possible: this is not a restaurant, it is a family room.

One of the issues raised with me during interviews was the importance of bathroom design and maintenance to dignity and respect. It is ideal for every bedroom to have its own washing facilities and toilet, but baths (especially those that need space and hoists) are likely to be shared. These therefore need to be carefully sited so that people do not have a long trek in a dressing gown; they should also be decorated as you would expect in a family home, not as a hospital facility.

Gardens for the soul

The importance of a garden to spiritual wellbeing cannot be overestimated. I have observed wonderful, imaginative gardens in the homes I visited, some with playful areas decorated like beaches or old movie sets, some with mini-orchards, one with statuary of figurines dedicated to past pets.

However, if there is not the space or willing volunteers to create an extravagant garden, then there are three things that are so much appreciated as to be essential: a water feature, a summerhouse (heated for all seasons) and flowerbeds with paths that are easy to navigate for the less mobile.

The more the garden and house merge together, the better for encouraging fresh air and mobility and avoiding claustrophobia. Not only are garden rooms and summerhouses very beneficial, but also semi-covered courtyards and 'open' corridors with French doors that can be fixed back in the summer and maximise light in the winter.

Family meals

At least one shared meal a day is approaching essential for physical and emotional wellbeing, but in making such an assertion it is important to recognise that there can be a problem of perception about this concept. Older people moving out of their own home, where they may have been isolated or meals have become erratic due to memory or care issues, often instinctively dislike being asked to sit with others at set times. Again the regimentation of the workhouse rears its ugly head, and relatives may take the same view, objecting to their loved ones being expected to conform and lose an element of independence.

It is necessary to see the issue from another point of view: families where meals are shared flourish, because the ritual creates space for interaction and addresses loneliness and depression. Older people say that once they have experienced this arrangement, they appreciate not only the company, but also the routine that builds punctuation into the day and week. The shared meal will normally be lunch, as people like to wake and dress in their own time, and generally wish to eat less in the evening.

Communal meals also stimulate appetite, and older people who had lived alone existing on tea and biscuits or microwaved meals can be observed to improve in physical and mental health once enjoying regular hot meals, home cooked and nutritionally balanced. Meals may be served by or shared with staff and managers, depending on the way the home is run, and this provides a regular opportunity for unobtrusive observation of residents during conversation.

Similarly, morning coffee and afternoon tea provide the same benefits. These can be at set times, with attendance optional, but they are most enjoyed when there is an element of ritual: sitting down together in the lounge or around a tea table. This is a very different scenario from a tea trolley being wheeled around, and even motivates some residents to put on a different dress in the afternoon specifically for the tea occasion. However, hot drinks and snacks should always be available to reinforce a sense of independence, both by providing galleys or coffee stations that people can use when they want and means to store food and prepare drinks in personal accommodation (with some exceptions that will be raised in a later chapter).

Governance and management

Residential homes and sheltered housing may be owned and managed in a number of ways, as the statistics in the earlier part of this chapter indicate. Much of the provision in the UK is on a commercial basis, either sold direct to residents or to local authorities, and some is still provided by statutory bodies. Charities are also a key player, and may have their roots in a faith tradition; these include MHA (previously Methodist Homes), Anchor and the Abbeyfield Society. The last of these was founded by Richard Carr-Gomm in 1956 as a result of his observing the degradations of loneliness amongst the elderly, and initially buying one house to enable a small number of people to live together in a community arrangement.

While commercial provision will be run by a business for the financial benefit of owners or shareholders, and charities will be governed by charitable law and objectives, their legal status should ideally not affect the interface between management and residents, the nature of which profoundly affects the wellbeing of older people and their carers. As with the physical building, management arrangements must be designed to create and favour relationships of mutual support. The nature of these, and the critical role of the manager as a catalyst within this paradigm, are explored in depth in Chapter 7.

The management structure needs to allow the manager (this can be a shared role) a high degree of autonomy in terms of organising schedules, deciding when to make short- or long-term operational changes to facilitate good interaction, dealing with maintenance and decoration matters, overseeing all aspects of mealtimes and nutrition and observing the wellbeing of residents. Autonomy goes with accountability, and demands a delicate balance of oversight: the manager needs to feels supported and be given positive reference points, but in the background there must be mechanisms that allow for control and discipline in the event they are needed. Where the home is a charity, or part of a group run by a charity, the Trustees are ultimately responsible and will have a vital role in maintaining a sound organisation that serves its residents and staff well. This means that they also form part of the web of relationships. In the case of a business, this role falls to the CEO and Board, which may raise conflicts of interest.

The manager of the home or housing will naturally be involved in paperwork and administration, including recruitment, health and safety, local budget control and purchasing decisions. Because his or her primary duty is to ensure a relational family, some managers deal with this by keeping paperwork 'in the background', while others may part-delegate it to an assistant or a volunteer.

Volunteers can play numerous roles in the life of the home. Many just wish to befriend residents, listen to them, help with outings or offer crafts and games. Others are committed to the organisation but prefer to stay in the background, and such people can be very important in freeing the manager's time to be on the frontline. Volunteers may be found or present themselves for many reasons, and in some homes there is a fluidity: retired staff volunteer, volunteers become residents and the family of deceased residents stay on and volunteer. In addition to their time and experience, one of the major benefits of volunteers is that they help maintain links between the life of the home and its local community.

Is there an ideal size?

The concept of the 'relational home', taking as its paradigm the family (warts and all), has grown out of the model of the original Abbeyfield homes, which were in general large family houses converted to accommodate somewhere around 8 to 12 people and a housekeeper. Many of the longer-established homes remain at this sort of size, although they may be grouped under a single charitable Trust rather than each being autonomous. New developments can be much larger with in excess of 50 apartments, both for sale and rent, and a wide range of facilities such as film rooms, gyms and beauty salons.

The dynamics of family relationships seem to adapt to various models, however. In smaller homes, each person will of necessity be in some sort of relationship with every other person, leading to a higher level of understanding but also a potentially more serious problem if one person is 'difficult'; managers spoke of having to act as mediators in this event. Much larger independent living developments tend to act as mini-villages, with people viewing each other as neighbours, and the family bonds forming between those who identify with others as like-minded or with interests in common. In this case, the role of the manager undergoes a subtle change, and they move into a position of overseeing the environment to ensure it favours bonding, but does not become part of any particular family group. Some carers, however, will move into these closer relationships.

Whilst not all older people will be able to choose the type of care into which they move, it is ideal if they can find a place in a home which suits their individual approach to life, and their own circumstances, either becoming part of a neighbourhood or of a family.

Finding a sense of belonging

Regardless of personal circumstances and choices, one's physical and mental wellbeing, ability to find meaning in life and spiritual contentment are all more likely to be improved by a sense of belonging and security. As I hope is becoming apparent from the observations described in this book, contentment and security are more than attainable in older age, even for those who have lost family and friends, if they can live in an environment designed to foster good relationships and optimise health status.

This desirable state of affairs can be quite fragile, and may be becoming more so. In a traditional intergenerational family, its younger members will arrive, grow and move on, and its older members will eventually die. This progression means that there is always a parental core, although the individuals forming this change with the generations. In a 'family' created within a residential home, the development is very different, with arrivals already mature and departures much more frequent and decisive. The longer each resident stays, and the more stable the management and staff, the more opportunity there is for bonds of trust to form and for people to relate to one another's roles and personalities. There is no doubt that this can work successfully, but the shorter the time each person is there, the harder it is for the community to flourish and individuals to benefit.

It is my observation that residents (and staff on their behalf) dread moving on to a care home or hospital more than they fear death. Indeed, residents told me that they felt they had a right to 'die at home' and this was now their home. This situation is exacerbated by the statutory requirement to reassess and readmit residents being paid for by Social Services after a period of hospitalisation leading to a delay and making it harder to re-integrate.

It is not easy to address this issue, but it could be ameliorated in at least two ways. One is to encourage older people to move into supported or residential accommodation before they are driven to it, such that they can reap the benefits and become part of a family while they still have the energy and will to do so. Staying in a lonely and unsuitable house for too long erodes mental and physical health. The second would be to design new developments to integrate different types of care, such that there is continuity between the stages of progressive need.

Meanwhile, the people involved use their own initiative at a local level. Managers and staff take the time to visit residents in hospital, and to keep in touch with those who have moved to care homes. In some accommodation, particularly that for dementia patients, the home may collaborate with Macmillan Nurses or a local hospice to manage residents through to their death, such that they can die in their 'family home' with familiar faces and easy access for relatives to visit right to the end. Relatives and staff may also then give one another comfort in shared loss.

Catalysts for relational care

Those fortunate enough to have a good marriage or friendship often say that these do not just happen, but have to be worked at, demanding thought and time. In the same way, relationships in residential settings are not just happenstance. We have seen in the previous chapters how these can be favoured or impeded by environment, management, governance and practical issues, and what appears to work towards greater health and contentment. None of these matters are random; they must be guided and controlled, so there are questions as to who facilitates good whole person care and who has the power to enable such facilitation.

In some organisations that own homes for older people, spiritual care (insofar as it can ever be separated from physical and mental care) is taken very seriously, and may be mainly the province of a chaplain. In others, there can be reliance on a hope that local places of worship will cater for spiritual needs, perhaps by holding services in the residential home, making arrangements for residents to get to church or by offering visiting chaplaincy on a regular basis.

There is no single definition of chaplaincy, but in the UK it is generally accepted that a chaplain will be a person who has been ordained or similar in a faith tradition, and will have a regular presence in the institution they are serving. The OED defines 'chaplain' as 'a member of the clergy attached to a private institution'. As one example, Cambridge University Hospitals describes the role on its website thus:

> The basic role of the chaplain is to be involved with others in the provision of holistic care within the hospital community. 'Holistic care' is concerned with the whole person and includes not only a person's physical health but also their social, emotional and spiritual health and wellbeing. Chaplains are pastoral practitioners who seek to build a relationship of trust through compassionate presence and thereby offer help and support.[1]

1 https://www.cuh.nhs.uk/chaplaincy/role-chaplain

While this support includes 'providing information on faith traditions and access to resources and rituals', and 'serving as a religious resource', the emphasis is on care of the whole person irrespective of any faith or none, helping them 'to cope with the psychological, social and spiritual aspects of their illnesses and difficulties arising from them'.

Chaplains serve in a wide variety of situations, such as places of work and education, public bodies including armed forces and health providers. In the UK (unlike the US, for example) they are not frequently employees of the organisation they serve, although they may be, and are not expected to be non-denominational.

The practice of a faith in a care home, whether as an individual or through collective worship, may be important to many of the residents, some of whom, when asked about sources of spiritual support in difficult times, mention prayer and God. Keith Albans (Albans and Johnson 2013, p.175) notes that 'For some, the experience of entering a care home...can enable them to reconnect with a worshipping community, albeit an informal one', and this observation was reflected by a member of staff at Abbeyfield: 'Older people often turn back to God. I've witnessed that in a lot of people over the years. It's like life is nearly finished, and they're preparing themselves for death.'

However, although they may draw support from worship, older people rarely talk about clergy or chaplains as their main 'listeners'. When the possibility of a visiting chaplain was raised with interviewees the response was that it would need to be someone local who came frequently and regularly and was involved in the life of the home or it would be more disturbing than reassuring. The local priest was not necessarily seen in this role: 'The minister comes and gives us a nice little service every month, but I don't think I would talk to him about anything worrying,' said one resident.

Listeners are drawn from the circle of the home, and when this is further explored, it seems to be the case because others living in the same home are thought more likely to understand, or to have things in common. The 'arm's length' status of the chaplain, valued in, say, the workplace, is not in this case necessarily seen as an advantage.

To fulfil their role, a chaplain must build relationships of trust. Is there, then, a key part for a chaplain to play in helping bonds form in residential settings, and themselves being part of the web of relationships that supports flourishing? Some charities providing elderly homes are strongly committed to this approach, and employ chaplains to cover a geographical area, who will visit each home regularly and offer pastoral support to residents and staff. Others may rely more on local clergy to call in, some of whom may be closely linked to the home, for example in a Trustee position. For instance, this is particularly the case in Scotland where homes may have been set up in part with the assistance of the Church of Scotland and the Church and home may be in physical proximity.

However, whatever the arrangement, the chaplain will not be living within the 'family' community and must perforce function in a different way. They may well have a role, especially in travelling with an older person on their spiritual journey and possibly linking them into religious practice, but I believe it would be a mistake to see this role as being the prime facilitator of the relational home, or acting as a substitute for the 'family' that actively supports the older person.

These observations on catalysis and the formation of bonds must and do have a practical impact on the work of chaplains in housing and care homes where the residents and staff are not transient. When Abbeyfield appointed an internal chaplain for the first time, shortly after the findings of this study were presented, it chose to take a different approach, recognising that these observations on catalysis and the formation of bonds, must and do have a practical impact on the work of chaplains in housing and care homes where the residents and staff are not transient. Abbeyfield therefore sought someone who would help each community strengthen its internal bonds rather than 'parachute' into all of them occasionally, such that they could support the managers in their critical role.

The Revd Edward Pogmore was the first person to be appointed, and following three years in the position he then took on the role of mentoring other Abbeyfield chaplains, basing his practice in part on the findings of the study cited in this book. As he explains:

> Right from the start of developing Chaplaincy staff support, integral to it was the encouraging of House and Care Home Managers to strengthening links with local churches and all faith communities, with faith leaders being invited in to learn more about Abbeyfield and how the whole care needs of the individual can be met in part from the local community.

> The nature of the chaplaincy service I have developed includes encouraging the discipline of Reflective Practice while addressing challenging pastoral situations such as end of life and bereavement care. This has been done through mixed role groups as part of the Abbeyfield Strategy. Chaplains work closely with their Divisional Management teams to ensure support to staff, so that they can work in a relational and purposeful way. Whole care assessment of residents takes time and can be challenging, and we can be a resource to staff as part of this process.
>
> Additionally, Chaplains consult with the development team in the planning of new schemes, in particular on the quiet rooms and reflective gardens that enhance and facilitate the spiritual and whole care values of Abbeyfield, as well as being involved in embedding these even further in staff induction.

Observing the interactions in residential settings where older people appear to be doing well, it seems that there must be a network of relationships, and that these can and need to be facilitated by a person who is both a daily participant in them and also has the ability to influence the overall environment. This person can only be the manager (or equivalent) and that role is considered in depth later in this chapter.

Turning first to the way in which the relational home operates, I have called this concept 'mutual chaplaincy'. The paradigm relies not on the traditional idea that some people are care-givers and some are receivers, but on the obvious truth that care must flow in both directions between two people. This may seem aspirational if care is identified only or primarily as physical assistance with hygiene, food, provision of activities and so on. But it is obvious when one considers the family model that care and love are about much more than this. Care is about listening, accepting, giving back of oneself in such a way that both people feel more understood or fulfilled than either was at the outset of the interaction. Viewed in this way, it can be seen that older people in 'care' can give, and that those with them who are younger and more physically able can receive. Similarly, two older people interacting can experience two-way care through conversation, listening and performing small acts of kindness that are normal to the human condition. This need not be demanding or sacrificial, but simply part of common life.

Because our proposition is that emotional and physical security is of prime importance to older people, and that this is grounded in relationships comparable to family bonds, the model must of necessity be different from that prevailing in other groups that are non-self-selecting, such as school or workplace. In those situations, people will normally find ways of interacting positively, but not be overly-reliant on the relationships unless they develop into self-selected friendships. In the care home, some residents may have family members but not necessarily close at hand or even close, so are far more reliant on staff, other residents and possibly volunteers, none of whom they actively chose to live with.

The care home manager

So what happens to help the family bonds form, when indeed they do, which is not inevitable? The part played by environment, norms and attitudes has already been explored, but the role of the home's manager is arguably the most critical, both in creating the environment and acting as a catalyst for 'mutual chaplaincy'. They must set the tone, ensure that loving kindness can be expressed and acted out, be a mediator in times of conflict, decide what is tolerable and tolerated on a daily basis and what needs escalated action. This person requires a high degree of autonomy backed by support and development from the management or Trustees of the organisation, and a form of oversight that is positive but recognises where ultimate accountability lies.

This analysis might raise the question as to whether such paragons can be found. Clearly, they can, as hundreds of care homes and many thousands of staff and residents benefit from their presence, but it takes wise governance of a charity or business to recognise them, help them reach their full potential, and value them through fair pay, training and compassionate monitoring. This approach to all staff results in better retention and a secure and sustainable business model from which all participants can benefit.

Arguably in well-functioning homes there are two relational models running side by side, complementary and harmonious: one is the model of good employment and care provision practice, the other is the model of the 'family'. So we see that both can blend together, for example, trustees overseeing the governance may become part of the 'family'; more than one spoke of seeing the manager of a home as a 'daughter'. There is also a blurring of lines between residents and volunteers insofar as the former may also take the role of the latter in terms of helping, listening, offering a lift to someone who doesn't have the bus fare, and in some larger homes taking a role such as running the shop or teaching a skill. This is very beneficial in helping people feel fulfilled and recognised as part of the social fabric.

One example of the critical part played by the manager as catalyst for mutual chaplaincy can be seen in issues relating to death and bereavement. During the interviews we considered how residents handled bereavement (and were helped in doing so), how it affected staff, what approach was taken to sharing news of loss and whether there was any opportunity for communal recognition.

How is spiritual life sustained in the face of death, where some people may have a profound faith and others none? Staff and managers generally felt that residents were reluctant to dwell on death when it occurred in the home. It is hard to establish if this is due to stoicism, or expectation that it would happen with increasing frequency, or to fear of the subject. Almost certainly, all these suppositions would apply to different people, some of whom were seen as 'taking it in their stride' and 'being fairly philosophical', while others did not wish to dwell on it: one manager said, 'Some shy away from it and don't want to think about it, others want to talk a lot.' However, it does not seem that most residents feel they are just 'sitting in St Peter's waiting room' or actively wish to hasten death. Indeed, there is more often a determination to enjoy what can be enjoyed. Given the age of the residents, which in many homes is on average above 90, it is interesting to wonder whether these people still draw on the stoicism engendered by World War 2; it is almost as though they are living in a war zone again, knowing that death may be imminent, but not wanting to waste time thinking about it.

A comment made by another manager raises the question of whether there is fear of death, or of the process of dying, both of which are understandable but different: 'Some are very frightened [of death], but I've also known many residents who have organised their funerals. They feel they've lived their life and see it as the next step.' This person also mentioned that a benefit of living in a sheltered house, as opposed to being alone at home, was the opportunity to talk about these fears and express one's wishes in advance.

However, there is a major difference in the attitudes of older people when the death is in their close family rather than in the home. This can affect them very much, and they may need to talk about their loss for some time. A volunteer reported the 'devastation' of a resident who lost her sister. Yet I spoke to another resident whose sister had died, and she had not told anyone in the home, because she could not bear any possible 'fuss'. Many of the residents who had died were already widowed and had moved into the home after the loss of a partner. Looking to the future, there may different issues in newer homes where there are more couples and one will predecease the other.

Residents want to remember others as they were, not to visit them for their last days in hospital, and often do not wish to go to funerals, although they may be offered and helped to do so in many homes. The emotional reluctance is almost certainly exacerbated by the physical problems of sitting on a pew for a length of time. They spoke of remembering and celebrating people in small ways, such as when that person's favourite cake was served and writing of them in the newsletter. In one home, they have an 'angel tree' at Christmas, decorated with an angel for each lost resident.

Conversely, managers nearly always wish to attend funerals, partly on their own account, partly to show care for the family and partly because residents like to have a report back rather than go themselves. In a few cases homes would organise the wake, but in general that was thought to be something the family wished to do and residents spoke of supporting the bereaved in small ways when they had to clear out their relative's room.

Staff recognise that residents may well grieve but not show it in a conventional manner, perhaps becoming unlike themselves, being touchy or aggressive for a while. This is seen as indicating an increased need for vigilance and care.

The impact of death in the home may fall more on the staff; two different volunteers I spoke to observed this. One said, 'Older people...don't get so emotionally involved with the loss of another, but staff do get upset,' and the other, 'Old people can cope much better, but the staff take it badly, because they're very caring.'

Managers recognise this, taking the role of facilitating 'mutual chaplaincy', but are likely themselves to be still struggling with losing residents 'because they are like your family'. They need in turn to draw on support in order to play the role, and primarily they cite staff turning to each other during times of grief, as well as talking to their line or area managers. Most importantly, being able to share with their own families is critical to a number. Although 'family' relationships are as ever the main source of support, where homes have instituted bereavement training this is welcomed and would seem to be good practice. One resident I spoke to suggested that, 'In a home where people have the capability, residents could set up a group to help the bereaved [members of staff].'

Snapshot: An empty bench

Rose, the manager of the home, is showing me around the garden courtyard onto which all the residents' rooms open. The French windows of some are ajar to let in the morning, others still closed and curtained. One has its windows wide open and furniture is being moved out. The lady who lived there died recently, and her rooms are being made ready for another. I ask Rose how people cope when they lose one of the community – and in particular, how does she cope? She answers that it's part of life: 'I don't really mourn. It's to be expected, the average age here is 94. I won't say no one feels it, of course they do, but I carry on and think of the next person who will be here.' We appreciate the fruit trees already offering their apples to people and wasps alike, and Rose indicates a particular wooden bench. 'She loved sitting there,' she says, and unobtrusively finds her handkerchief.

Where managers have a faith, this also is of great help to them, death being accepted as part of the continuum of life within their belief system, and their faith providing them with the ultimate and unfailing sustenance of God.

Although the ability of managers to bring people together and help them cope is critical, and must inevitably draw on their personal resources, few express any desire to avoid this role; rather, it was seen as being integral to membership of the 'family'. One said she liked people to die in the home rather than in hospital, as she would be sure their last days had been happy; staff report that residents are frightened of going into hospital and ask to die at home, and that observation is strongly supported by my interviews with residents. One manager said: 'People will see how the dying are treated as a sign of what will happen to them, respect and care are essential.'

Managers also have to decide and mediate how news of a death is given to residents, and in this respect there was a marked divergence between different homes. This in itself indicates that managers are judging the nature, size and cohesion of their 'family', and deciding what will be best for it.

Some deliberately announce a loss to the whole community at the same time, normally at a meal, to avoid uncertainty spreading and to be able to observe reactions to judge who might need further support. In other homes, there is an equally deliberate choice to tell each resident separately: 'You have to give them the information at the right time – if it may upset them, and you need time to sit with them. It's never announced.'

It is worth noting, first, that the method used is not related to the size of the home. In one larger home, everyone was told individually the morning after. In several smaller homes, an announcement was made at the next meal. In one home, they told close friends first then made a general announcement. Second, the approach taken has in all cases been thought through by the manager and chosen for good reasons. All homes believed they were being sensitive to residents' needs, and most were, but perfection is impossible and death a very difficult issue and just one resident said, 'It's hit and miss what you find out.'

Death and bereavement in the home, and the way they are handled, provide a practical example of how 'mutual chaplaincy' manifests organically and the role of the manager in facilitating its operation. It also illustrates the way in which the greatest burden can fall on the manager, and their general response when asked how they coped. They turn to those closest: staff, residents and their own family. The only source of support mentioned as desirable but largely absent was interaction with the managers of other homes, and there is an expressed need to understand and learn from 'how things were done' elsewhere.

Managers mediate to ensure relationships flourish and foster peaceful living and there is no doubt that their role is recognised as critical by staff and residents. They act as the catalyst that enables relationships, as well as participating in them; a Trustee noted this in practical terms: 'When she's not here, there's no one to say, come on let's get together.'

Speaking at a meeting of the Spirituality Forum (27 January 2014), the former Archbishop of Canterbury, Rowan Williams, posed the question: 'How can you prepare people for a job that is never done? When there are no boxes to tick?' He suggested that those whose work was care for others may develop a notion of 'fidelity', a sense of reward that is to do with staying with the role and situation, rather than with completion of a task.

Fidelity of the type expected from managers would seem to demand a high level of emotional and spiritual support, yet during interviews with managers no one spontaneously mentioned feeling the need for pastoral care; some accessed this from visiting clergy or the local church, but mainly, the need was not felt so long as internal networks of support were strong – the beneficial circle of care referred to earlier. In larger homes where there are staff whose dedicated role is to listen and befriend, this does not preclude the 'family' model forming and operating and may enhance it.

A similar situation pertains to staff when expressing need for spiritual or emotional support; there may be different levels of need depending on the person and their experience, but similar responses in terms of sources of support. They saw the relationships as both demanding and sustaining, saying for example, 'I've always given a lot of myself, so it's a natural thing, it's not hard to do' and 'I feel as much as I give them [the residents], I always get something back.'

Nevertheless, it must be recognised that this is a demanding job for staff at all levels in a home, and that they 'take on certain people's feelings, problems, emotions,' as one cleaning assistant said when she related sometimes feeling 'drained'. Managers are the most frequent source of support for staff, with other colleagues also playing an important part, as well as trustees and volunteers if they are seen as accessible, which really means being in the home frequently and being part of its life. No one suggested this internal network had let them down, and many used the word 'trust' to explain how it worked for them.

CHAPTER 6

DEMENTIA HOMES

What distinguishes the relationships that form in dementia homes?

The statistics presented in Chapter 1 indicate the growing prevalence of older people living with dementia; whether this will continue to increase on the same trajectory will be affected by a number of factors, including prevention and treatment regimes about which we can only speculate at present. It would seem natural to assume that the relational home and the concept of 'mutual chaplaincy' would either not be applicable to dementia homes, or would be very difficult to realise, given that it appears to rely on building understanding, sustained interaction and trust.

My work with Abbeyfield, however, suggests that very similar basic issues and principles apply in dementia homes as in others, and their interpretation into practice is not radically different but does have specific implications for staffing, environment and overall governance. Dementia homes in which people are thriving in one way or another do in fact create a coherent 'family', an assertion supported by comments from staff such as: 'We are a family, it's not an institution' and 'The essence of this home is that we are a happy family.'

Hearing the voices of older people with dementia, and honouring what they say, demands a different but not necessarily more difficult approach to listening. For example, asking if someone is happy will not return a direct or consistent response, but during the course of a conversation, it is certainly possible to sense one or more prevailing emotions and assess whether a person is at peace in their environment, whether they feel a sense of purpose and whether they are relating positively to others around them.

Conversations may be 'circular' in that people want to reiterate certain points, and will therefore answer any lead question by returning to that point. In some cases, the point of return itself can be informative and indicate something about mood; for example, one lady enjoyed explaining how she had moved on from a violent relationship in a very satisfying way. People who suffer falls (which may have been the reason for entering the home) will frequently recount the story of the fall, which clearly has a profound effect on them.

In understanding how older people with dementia feel about their lives in a home, and trying to gauge quite elusive matters such as peace of mind and fulfilment, it is important to bear in mind that the mood articulated in a discussion may not tally with the apparent state of affairs, because people are moving between different realities. For example, one person may say she is 'nervous' of the staff, because they watch her, but when encountering a carer may appear happy and relaxed in their company. To give another example, a lady sat at the piano and played beautifully, but when showed a flash card indicating music as an activity said she did not enjoy it.

Creating relationships

Given that residents may be living in different realities, and that this may change in the course of the day, the question must arise as to whether they are able to form the relationships that have been identified as being so essential to wellbeing.

First, it must be acknowledged that the very fact of having companionship available can be a great positive to many residents: people say things such as, 'The company's nice, people are nice' and 'Just people walking around [make it] interesting'.

Episodes of frustration or unhappiness that residents describe seem to be counterbalanced by company; when they speak of people being around their demeanour can be seen to improve. The fact of others being in the room not only cheers people, but they also see company as part of the safety offered by the environment, and contributing to a sense of being comfortable. One summed this up: 'People are so friendly, that makes it,' and another, 'All the house [are my friends] I would say'.

For some residents, specific friendships are very important: 'You make a special friend who you talk to more than others. That's life, isn't it?'

When asked, 'What's important to you?' answers such as, 'My friends are important to me' and 'You have to look in corners to find them' (talking about making special friends) were given.

It may seem hard to reconcile these avowals with the observation that those same people did not appear to know the names of their friends or remember much about them. However, this is not a dissonance, as residents with dementia will clearly recognise and go to be near a friend, drawn by a memory that they enjoyed being with that person, even if they may not remember exactly the nature of the enjoyment.

Interestingly, the same people who talk of the value of friendship will sometimes seem less certain about their relationships and balance a very positive statement with a negative, for example that not everyone likes them, or that they do not really want to be intimate. If someone is in the mood to be private, they may interpret this as a lack of friendship on the part of others, but the important point is that the home should be organised to provide the possibility of friendship.

The influence of current 'age'

Because those with dementia experience different 'ages' at different times, staff can make them feel more secure by recognising that residents' roles may shift during the day and responding appropriately. For example, someone may feel they are the elder of the family at one 'now' in the day, and the child of the family at another time.

Similarly, there can be ambiguity in relating to visiting relatives, perhaps because of an uncertainty about what age the resident is experiencing themselves as being at the time. People may initially 'know' a visitor, but not be sure if or how they are related, and relatives need reassurance from carers that it is worth staying and allowing time: 'I don't know who is who sometimes when they come in. Then I gradually know who they are.' Enabling people to recognise a visitor gives a sense of self; and where a home is based in a small-town community, and old friends can come in, this also helps give a sense of continuity and meaning to life.

Residents live in a current present, which may not be externally consistent but is 'real'; this may not cause distress, but questioning it can be counterproductive to sense of self.

Snapshot: Playing a part

Maria is quite tall, and has retained an air of elegance, although she walks slowly and even hesitantly as she shows me around her home. We appreciate all the things that are there to be appreciated: the colourful hats on stands for residents to pick up, wear and discard; the re-creation of a village post office with sweets and scales, when sweets are suddenly in demand. In one of the lounges is a semi-grand piano. Maria sits at it and plays. The music is wonderful, a flowing sonata purely from memory. Her carer and I listen, and others come and stand around, briefly silent. The music lasts for maybe five minutes, magical in a room that is often restless. Residents drift away. Maria suddenly closes the piano lid. 'I mustn't', she says. 'I mustn't play any longer, my father will tell me off, he gets angry if I play too long.'

Memories of the past

As with all older people, sharing memories is another vital aspect of giving meaning to current life. While this can happen spontaneously, if the older person has dementia there is a particular need to record memories more formally than may be appropriate in a non-dementia home, to ensure relevant episodes and preferences are kept up to date in the care plan. However, there are some caveats concerning this, which are addressed later in the chapter.

For people without dementia, reminiscence and 'making sense of life' are often very important, and this process of imbuing life with meaning happens by talking over personal and communal history, remembering incidents around themes such as marriage and work, and so on. But there is not a universal desire to dwell on the past, and people also enjoy talking about future plans and expectations, such as proposed outings.

Managers and staff who are alert to the need to capture memories find that there is a continual balance to be struck between supporting and drawing on reminiscence and determinedly talking about the past when people may be more at peace in their present. Some (not all) people with dementia do recognise that they have problems with remembering the past, but (as indeed is the case with those who do not have dementia), they are divided as to how much they wanted to actually spend time doing this.

When memories have become uncertain, or are no longer sequential, does spiritual fulfilment require a different approach to capturing these? Where people with dementia are concerned, the process cannot happen in the same way, as memories are not 'ordered' and are being explored as they arise, so the listener has to respond to each in the present moment. The person themselves may have other ways of finding meaning, for example, by processing thoughts during 'circular walking'.

An additional complication is that past experience may overshadow current enjoyment. One example was a lady who liked the food, but said, 'You have to eat it carefully', referring to her childhood experience of being drilled in table manners; another liked feeding the guinea pigs, but was scared they would escape and she would be reprimanded by her teacher.

Addressing problems that occurred in the past, with the aim of reducing current pain, can be very difficult, as it may have the opposite effect to that intended, by recreating pain in the 'now' of the person. It requires considerable time and specialist knowledge.

Some residents with dementia derive more enjoyment from going through *other* people's memories rather than their own: I found that there could be a lot of conversation and questions stimulated by a scrap book belonging to one of the interviewers, without it necessarily evoking confidences from the interviewee. This bears out John Killick's observation (2013) that items relating to a person's own memories may not always be the best way to elicit conversation, and a piece of 'memory neutral' music or art may be as effective. I noticed that there was also an issue of phraseology: a suggestion of 'talking about the past' seems to result in a more positive reaction than a suggestion of 'sharing memories', possibly because the latter can feel more intrusive and hence threatening.

There needs to be a balance where reminiscence is concerned: while capturing memories may help to meet a person's current needs better or remind them of past joy, if residents are happy living in the present, they may be unconsciously protecting themselves from sorrow that cannot now be ameliorated or put into a longer term perspective.

Snapshot: After the fall

Elaine looks frail, and her hand is small and dry in mine as we are introduced in the breakfast room. She smiles, frowns and looks down at the floor anxiously. 'I had a fall last week, I don't know what happened, I was just standing and then the floor came up at me, and now I'm really bruised.' I listen as she describes the feeling of falling, lives through it again.

Janice, one of the care workers, joins us. She is going to sit in on the interview, as agreed with Elaine's daughter. Slowly, quite peaceably, we walk down the corridor, take the lift to Elaine's room, get settled down. She moves uncomfortably in her chair, raising her trouser leg to show me bruises. 'I had a fall last week, the floor came up and hit me, I don't know how it happened.' Janice hugs and reassures her that it's over now, she is getting better, she's safe now.

I ask about the pictures, the battered ornament of the Virgin Mary, the books. We look through her life story scrapbook, and the questions I need to ask weave into the pauses and recollections of the previous years and moments. Elaine's hands rest in her lap. A short silence, and then 'I had a fall last week, I don't know what happened…'

The relationship with faith

Some dementia homes provide Christian services by a church that historically has links with the home, or other faith celebrations of some sort, and staff report that when residents attend these, they seem to make a particular connection through the music and singing elements.

Residents may keep religious artefacts in their rooms, or photographs of churches, but although they appear to be precious to their owners in that they have clearly been kept a long time, their significance can be rather vague. For example, a lady had a carving of The Last Supper, which she could not identify but knew 'was something special to me'. Asked if she had a religion, she said it did not play an important part in her life. Relationships with religion can be uncertain or ambiguous: asked 'Are you religious?' one resident answered, 'Not now, I don't, I'll have to do it again so I will.'

However, what one might call the 'cultural memory' of religion seems to evoke much stronger feelings. Clearly for many elderly people, attending church or Sunday School will have been an important part of their early lives, whether or not they had an active belief. They would remember: 'We went to Sunday School and sang about Jesus', 'When I was a child, I had to go to church'. The memories are not necessarily positive: 'I'm a Roman Catholic, I went to a convent school, I had it 24 hours a day, religion, religion, religion.' It seems that religious practice forms a significant part of the memory bank for better or worse.

How family bonds operate in dementia homes

The importance of friendship, and of feeling one is amongst friends, has already been cited as vital to the comfort and security of the home environment. This is akin to living in a family: 'It's like a home from home', 'It's like one big, massive family'. The bonds may form in dementia homes in different ways from those in other types of accommodation, and residents may be less consciously aware of them, but this does not diminish their significance to wellbeing. One interviewee summarised to me: 'I would say it is the bond that is created between the staff and the residents here, and also residents with other residents – that's the key.'

Sense of self

Helping each other improves a 'sense of self', and the benefits of fostering self-worth have been explored in previous chapters, not only with reference to the value of people having tasks and roles, but also their need for quiet spaces where there can be one-to-one conversations, during which, as a carer said, 'People can express their sense of self much better.'

To achieve this, while there must be sensible risk-assessment, the life of the home cannot be too constrained by risk; residents should be encouraged to 'be themselves' at whatever 'age' they are currently experiencing, for example by doing jobs they feel drawn to, looking after themselves and others. Sense of self is also nurtured by giving choice and control over, for example, when to get dressed, eat or wash, what to wear or what activities to participate in.

The creation of family bonds and relationships is key to an environment that protects dignity, security and sense of self, and people describing this mentioned the importance of knocking on doors before entering, sensitivity over physical contact and talking to residents for a while before helping them with personal care. As with all aspects of dementia care, touch – which is a vital way of communicating – takes considerable care time in terms of being introduced gradually, and then used consistently, for example by sitting holding hands.

In the same way that maintaining the balance between privacy and company is critical in other types of home, so in dementia homes the balance between creating a feeling of independence and of security is important and challenging, and requires that the managers and staff are given as much local discretion as possible to get the balance right for that particular home at any one time.

The life of the home cannot be a series of tasks, and this is recognised by homes that are nurturing: 'Care is not a question of tasks, it must be more holistic.' Similarly, it is important not to do tasks for people which they could do for themselves, or to be too quick to complete sentences and find words for them.

The way that the life of the home is conducted must continually be referenced back to the individual concerned. Flexibility of provision (food, activities and so on) gives people more control and hence more sense of self, while change and transition need preparation and discussion such that they remain within the control of those affected as much as possible; people who feel rushed or coerced will not recover peace of mind quickly.

Listening and attentiveness

Family bonds cannot form without conversation, which happens both between residents and with their carers. Although carers must engage with residents as they undertake tasks, the listening needs to be more focused and purposeful than in non-dementia homes. In the latter, very important interchanges can happen while tasks are undertaken, but in dementia homes, there may be times when attention needs to be undivided and information needs to be formally recorded.

For example, over the summer of 2017 the Cambridge Housing Society (CHS) set up a small-scale pilot intergenerational housing project to provide accommodation for postgraduate students in one of its sheltered schemes at reduced rents in return for volunteering and spending time with elderly residents. Existing residents were consulted on a collective and individual basis on the project proposal, with an overall positive response after some initial reticence. Three postgraduates have been selected and trained in partnership with the Cambridge Hub, which engages Cambridge University students in practical local volunteering projects. They have been recording time spent on activities with residents including befriending, running errands, preparing meals, film nights, trips and administrative activities such as meetings and student training in data protection, dementia awareness and so on.

A methodology to measure developed by the project team, combining the Warwick-Edinburgh NHS wellbeing approach with the Campaign to End Loneliness surveys, will measure impact on a quarterly basis against a baseline survey. In response to wide interest in the project from across housing and other sectors, CHS and the Cambridge Hub will be running briefings and workshops, to share experience and learning from the initial six months.

Because residents may be experiencing different parts of their lives at different times of the day, reminiscence in a sense is continuous. However, this process has to differ from that noted in other types of housing, where staff will actively evoke or discuss memories. In dementia homes the process has to be taken slowly with particular care to respect a strong disinclination to delve back into the past.

Distractions need to be avoided, but artefacts to stimulate conversation are very useful. For example, where there is a TV, it seems to be more of an intrusion that draws the eye, rather than something that people actively watch; large TVs in a central position do not favour listening, but placed in a smaller secondary lounge may promote some conversation.

The part played by managers and staff

It is obvious from these observations how critical the staff of the home are to all aspects of wellbeing of the residents and of each other. Managers say it is important to appoint on the basis of empathy, to watch and judge how candidates relate to residents before making a hiring decision to ascertain as much as possible if they are 'prepared to join in with everything: singing, dancing, humour and laughter' and able to 'tune in'. In effect a new member of staff is joining the 'family' of the home and needs ready access to local management to get involved quickly and to be able to talk about problems, in particular if residents are difficult or abusive, and the emotions this challenge evokes.

It is essential to the wellbeing of all that staff are capable of empathy and enabled to express love, as they will have a critical effect on the nature and spiritual life of the home. Training can assist in the practical expression of care, and there is a requirement to supply this and encourage its uptake, but as one wise manager observed: 'You cannot train people to love, but you can train them how best to show love.'

It is therefore all the more important that managers have control over local decisions that may impact on residents' wellbeing, such as the ability to adapt rotas in consultation with staff, and to commission simple repairs locally, especially when these affect daily life.

The part played by relatives and the community

Relationships that residents enjoyed when they were part of the local community can still be of great value to them after they move into a home, but these may be harder to sustain in the case of residents with dementia.

Insofar as relatives are concerned, managers note significant benefits from continued relationships between a resident and their family: 'When families visit regularly, I can see the difference it makes to residents.' In some cases this happens without too much effort on the part of the home; but in others it takes time and energy and even a struggle to promote contact. One way to do this is to ensure that relatives are positively welcomed and encouraged to treat the home as though it were their own, rather than as visitors. For example, they can be given the simple facility to make drinks for themselves in the kitchen, as though they were still in their loved one's house.

When 'meaningful visits' can be facilitated, for instance by having memorabilia around to discuss, or things to do such as games, then those visits will last longer and be more interactive. Suitable communal rooms with small private areas for conversation encourage people to stay longer. Conversely, large lounges with seats around the perimeter or loud TVs make intimacy harder.

Gardens are also important, providing areas where people can relax together, as are points of interest such a sweet shop, where children can go with grandparents.

Some families may cease visiting or do so reluctantly if they feel that they have already 'lost' their loved one, making being with them seem a pointless or even painful exercise. Homes can address this type of fear and misunderstanding through gentle 'training', which can be welcomed if given by those who care for their relative. Families can also reach a much more positive state of mind once their relative is settled in, as they no longer have to live with the guilt of trying to care and not fully succeeding, so relationships are seen to improve once the right home has been found.

One of the greatest problems occurs when residents are uprooted to be near family, losing their friends, but are then not visited regularly: 'This is really sad, they take them away from friends to be near the family, and then the family don't want to be involved.' The same type of problem arises if older people are moved out of their locality by their local authority, because it is seeking the least expensive care home option.

Losing ties with the local community can be a real deprivation. If residents feel they are still part of the community, who come in as visitors, volunteers or to use the facilities (for example for club meetings), it gives a feeling of purpose to the establishment; one can certainly notice the difference between homes that are 'buzzing' with visitors from nearby and those that are more isolated. This type of interaction is not just a function of being situated in a small town, as for instance 70 per cent of residents in one of the London homes I visited had been born locally.

Student volunteers are an exception, in that they seem to visit dementia homes more than is the case for non-dementia homes, volunteering for various reasons associated with their careers:

beauty students giving manicures, medical students requiring the experience, young people aiming for the Duke of Edinburgh Award. Those whose family members were in the home may help at the time, but are likely to be lost after the parent passes away. This results in a high level of transience, which in non-dementia homes would likely be a problem in terms of forming bonds, but dementia home managers note it is not negative because 'Residents like to see new faces, it cheers them up'.

However, longer-term volunteers can be very valuable in monitoring and noticing problems, which demands building trust and knowledge of the home, but they may be harder to find because the needs of the residents are perceived as being high.

Coping with loss of 'family' members

The dementia home 'family' seems to be less disrupted by loss and change than is the case in non-dementia homes, and more disrupted by people who are anxious or feel lost and show this by aggression or difficult behaviour. This can to an extent be addressed by seeking greater understanding of the person, and relatives have a role to play here in helping staff with information and insights about the person.

The death or departure of a resident does represent a point of change in the life of the home, but is unlikely to be an unusual occurrence or a shock, as there is an expectation that dementia homes will nurse residents until death as part of the overall care plan. Palliative care may be given by district or Macmillan nurses, or nurses from a local hospice coming in and working with the home's staff. There are implications for staff time, as someone must be available to sit with the patient almost constantly.

When there is a bereavement, the news must be given in such a way as to suit the recipient's cognitive ability, and while some residents may express grief, this is the exception, and it is normal for staff to mourn the loss much more. When a resident has had a nominated special carer, that person may feel the loss even more keenly than when the relationships were more general. The type of support sought at this time is overwhelmingly from others within the home. Staff and managers turn to each other for comfort and reminiscence, and one said of bereavement: 'Support from peers is the main feature.'

Comfort is also found by attending the funeral to say a formal goodbye (staff rotas may need to be adjusted so that those closest to the deceased can go) and from the appreciation expressed by the family of the person who has died. The latter can be very important, so if a family appears not to care too much, this will impact on staff as well.

It is when residents lose a close family member, without necessarily remembering the details of whom they have lost but being aware it has happened, that they most need support and suffer grief, and their health may deteriorate; for them this is a vital transition point that must be recognised.

Another transition point in the family life of the home is the permanent departure or arrival of staff, especially if close bonds have been formed over time, or between particular people. Residents can usually cope well with this if staff take time to talk to them about the change, explain what is happening and monitor and give extra attention to anyone who seems particularly disturbed by a loss. The presence of other residents who can express care for each other is one of the main ways that the stress of transitions is ameliorated.

The physical environment

Accommodation and decoration

As is the case with all shared housing for older people, the provision of smaller, quiet and peaceful communal rooms as opposed to one large lounge favours different pursuits and conversations and therefore contributes to wellbeing.

Communal areas need points of interest and reminiscence, and some homes such as those run by Abbeyfield offer excellent examples, with a wonderful variety of small rooms decorated as libraries, nurseries, shops and craft rooms, as well as living and dining rooms. Given their interest in being in company, it is likely that people prefer these areas to being in their own rooms, although it is not possible to be sure. Certainly, there will be considerable variation in how much people wish to personalise their bedrooms, some favouring a quantity of photographs, books and cuddly toys, while others are quite Spartan by choice.

It may be that there is a problem 'committing' to a room, if a resident believes they will leave soon. One lady said to me: 'I put my photos away, because I don't want to look at them. I like to see faces, not photos. I'll go [back home] sometime soon, this isn't home.' This lady said she was very happy about being in company, but was clearly not settled.

All the residents seem to agree on the importance of views, from communal rooms and particularly from their bedrooms: 'This window is a blessing.' The views appreciated and commented on are not generally those of nature, but of people and movement, such as visitors arriving, neighbours leaving their houses, people walking down the street, even the rubbish collection; and most of all, children at play.

'Circular walking routes' are needed and where there are artefacts to touch and look at, they will definitely receive attention from residents walking around. It is recognised that people with dementia may wish or need to walk around, and ideally this should be accommodated without barriers, but also without risk. Providing circular routes facilitates this need. For example, the Alzheimer's Society booklet 'Walking About' suggests 'having a circular path with points of interest...can make the experience more enjoyable' (Alzheimer's Society 2015, p.10).

Even more than is the case in other types of accommodation, staff in dementia homes put considerable emphasis on the equation of bathroom facilities with self-respect. Private showers and WCs were deemed essential, so that people did not have to rush or carry personal things in communal areas, which was 'not dignified'.

Gardens and nature

Abbeyfield has been developing a programme called 'A Breath of Fresh Air' with Dementia Adventure (2018). A pilot scheme in Epping, which enabled residents to get outside to connect with nature, indicated the potential of the approach. Abbeyfield's evaluation, after the pilot, showed that increasing the amount of time spent outside meant that the number of residents:

- who felt moderately lonely fell from 77 per cent to 11 per cent
- experiencing falls decreased by 10 per cent

- getting seven hours or more sleep a night increased from 55 per cent to 88 per cent
- rating their appetite as 'good' rose from 66 per cent to 100 per cent
- saying their mood was 'good' rose from 33 per cent to 66 per cent.

Research conducted by Rebecca Whear of the University of Exeter (Whear *et al.* 2014) indicates the benefits of 'sensory stimulation and an environment that triggers memories' (University of Exeter 2014), but also warns that staff time to help residents take full advantage of the outdoors is an essential.

New developments for older people can readily incorporate greening and wildlife, which is much valued by residents not only for its effect on mood, but also for the opportunities it provides to enjoy observing nature, whether by being outside or via webcams. The Wildlife Trusts have pioneered the integration of wildlife into new builds, working with developers, landlords and residents, and have many examples to share (Wildlife Trust, Summer 2017, pp.5–8).

Residents also relate to pets and animals, and will look at them, talk about them and sometimes want to feed them. There are ways that homes can promote this benefit, either by keeping pets if their welfare can be assured, bringing them in with owners, and having programmes such as 'living eggs' and garden camcorders.

Food and mealtimes

Mealtimes are one of the best opportunities to foster interaction, but there are some differences as to how dementia homes can best use this opportunity, as opposed to other types of housing. There needs to be more flexibility of timing, to accommodate people who want to get up late or are having a 'bad day', and also a greater choice of food provided. Although menus may be discussed with residents and planned ahead, there should be recognition that people may want something different on the day depending on their mood and present 'age', and where possible cooks should be enabled to meet this need. Equally, people appreciate being able to make or have a drink whenever they want. If times of meals and choice of food are as flexible as possible, residents have more control and more sense of 'self' and individuality.

The extent to which residents look forward to food and mealtimes is very variable (more so than in non-dementia homes), but given the enthusiasm for friendship and company, it is likely that meals are popular for this reason as much as any other. Nevertheless, managers and staff have no doubt that regular, hot, home-cooked meals improve nutrition and mood and help residents become more active and interactive.

'Mutual chaplaincy' in dementia homes

Those to whom I spoke in dementia homes were often quite clear about the changes they observed in residents after moving from their 'own' home and arriving in Abbeyfield – in some cases, in quite a short time. They were described as more alert, more interactive and more confident in being themselves. This was ascribed partly to the physical environment, with company around, regular nutrition and a greater variety of activities. However, it was also ascribed to forming bonds with staff and each other, and to no longer being rushed or judged, as they may have been when relatives or domiciliary carers were attempting to work through tasks. One manager said: 'People become more contented' and another: 'In certain instances it changes quite suddenly and significantly for the better...from being very tearful, to being content.'

What we see in dementia homes where people can be at their best is, again, the operation of 'mutual chaplaincy': a support system in which a group of disparate people become a connected community where life can be lived as richly as possible. Residents and staff will articulate this in various ways, as 'Being known', 'Feeling safe, knowing there is someone around' and 'Being who you want to be'.

Fostering good relationships, helping gently to keep them refreshed and positive, contributes to happiness and a feeling of security; where some senses are being lost due to the process of dementia, isolation becomes an increasing risk, and facilitating companionship all the more important.

However, in doing this staff have to adapt to the current 'now' of residents. Virtually all residents value company, but while sometimes they may initiate conversation, at other times it needs to be arranged by staff, for example by bringing together people whom they know share a common background or interest. Stimulation leads to interaction, as the emotions of friendship can be recollected but not necessarily the 'reasons' for the friendship. Because they may need to act as catalysts, there are more demands on staff time but it is not necessarily seen as burdensome.

The process of mutual chaplaincy can also encompass finding suitable ways for everyone to express their sense of self. Opportunities for playing a part in the home may be more limited, but it is possible to achieve the reassurance of personal value if people can do the tasks they wish to, for example, sharing a talent such as playing an instrument or re-finding a previous role such as home-making. One resident said she loved tidying up: 'I do, yes, I really do.'

Even more than in other types of home (where it is also very important) residents in dementia homes talk about enjoying jokes and laughter: 'We have good fun together' and 'I've got friends here, I pull their legs, that's my occupation.' Staff recognise this and are very much part of the activities rather than just organising them, thus nurturing bonds and providing the foundations for a supportive 'family life', and maintaining the continual fine balance between providing autonomy and security.

Implications for dementia homes

The observations made in this chapter indicate that, while the ethos and benefits of 'family living' can be applied equally in dementia homes as in other accommodation for the elderly, there needs to be adjustment to ensure the concept works well for residents and staff. Some things have to be done differently.

Recording memories

We have seen that when people have dementia, listening needs to be focused, and cannot necessarily take place during other tasks. This means that staff may have to think differently about how they listen to memories, and whether and how these might need to be recorded to help maintain understanding of a person's individuality. Memories do need to be formally noted for care plans where relevant and residents may welcome opportunities to talk about the past, but exploring memories together with others, especially staff, can open up pain or vulnerabilities, which it may already be too late to address. Sometimes it is more positive and enjoyable to enable people with dementia to talk about the memories and past of other people such as visitors and staff.

There is also the question of staff and residents getting to know about one another such that trust can be built. Memory boxes, relatives' stories and chats can all help a carer understand more about someone's past, and hence their present; recent evidence also suggests that making a short film of a person's life, using old photographs, loved music and public film clips, can not only help a mutual understanding when watched together, but can also decrease anxiety in the person with dementia.

When trying to judge what matters to residents and makes them content, it is important to recognise the disparity between what people say they like to do, which may be based on memories, and what they actually show pleasure in doing now. In her novel, *The Wilderness*, Samantha Harvey writes from the point of view of a protagonist Jake, who has increasing dementia. He sees a shoulder of beef in a food shop:

> He looks back at the beef, remembers a precise time when he had it in a sandwich with hot white sauce...the memory of this food is more real than the present, and in this memory he loves it – the taste and the warmth of the meat, the fondness of the moment. But that slab of pink meat...makes him feel sick now. (Harvey 2009, p.96)

There is a danger that simply recording memories may not have a real relevance to helping people to feel fulfilled as they are *now*, in the present. Another risk is that residents can be close to staff, but may also behave ambiguously if past memories affect current relationships. It is important to understand and note information about the person as they are in the present, even though memories may put that present in a wider context.

As memory becomes more challenging, care and activities need to be about providing joy and laughter 'in the moment', which demands time, empathy, and non-verbal communication; the home's capacity and training should accommodate this demand.

Handling transition

There are a number of points of transition and change that the 'family' of the home has to work through. Again, there is much that is common to all types of communities of older people, and some aspects that are specific to dementia homes.

One transition point occurs when the individual resident moves into the home, and the timing of this is critical in terms of subsequent wellbeing. The optimum approach is to plan ahead when the person is still able to take ownership of the decision, and hence feel more in control and less stressed. This is also better for the family as a whole and allows for preparation to be made, for example, deciding what should be taken to the home. Ideally, visiting the home for daytime activities first provides a way of staff getting to know people and vice versa, before the decision to move in is made.

However, the luxury of time is not always achievable. In some cases, people may move to the home from a hospital stay because they are no longer able to live independently and in others there may have been a crisis point that forced the move. Immediately after arrival, older people may well experience a 'dip' in wellbeing but then pick up and reach a state of mind that is more positive than before the move was made.

Some people will come to a dementia home from another form of elderly housing such as sheltered accommodation. They are likely in that case to have reached a point at which relatives, other residents or the manager believe the situation cannot continue and specialist care is needed.

This stage may be indicated by a number of practical problems, for instance when 'wandering' becomes too frequent and there are security issues, or other residents feel their personal space is being invaded.

Until this point is reached, there may be little desire on the part of residents or managers to see people with dementia forced to leave too soon, particularly in the rare cases where the person was or is the partner of another resident. In an ideal world, there would be a dementia care home nearby, so that the transition could be made in a considered manner, and without ties being broken. There is no reason why 'mixed' homes should not move towards becoming more dementia friendly, but it is vital to have a full consultation and engagement process for current residents and their relatives if this is to work; the question of mixed homes is explored in more detail later in this chapter.

Snapshot: Is it sharing when you don't have a choice?

Jean has always lived in Essex, and now she is seated – but not settled – in a large corner room of a care home in one of the county's small towns. Her bungalow is only round the corner and she intends to go back, in spite of the people who keep knocking on the windows and calling to her in strange voices. Is she uncomfortable? No. How is the food here? Very good. Indeed, she is looking far stronger already since she moved in. Jean loves sharing a conversation, but she is finding 'sharing' all her clothes, books and fruit very difficult. The other residents have dementia; they wander into her room, pick things up, use her bathroom and have to be guided away. Jean has lost none of her intelligence or somewhat acerbic humour over her 95 years, but this is beyond her. 'Why do people want to steal my things?' she ponders. 'It's really not right.'

Activities and outings

All the evidence from talking to residents and staff indicates that activities are important to residents' wellbeing, mentally, spiritually and physically. The greater the variety the better, to make sure that the needs of different types of people are met, and that there are things they can do alone and together. More than would be the case in non-dementia homes, it is necessary for staff to monitor who is enjoying what by watching body language, such as people tapping their feet to music.

Residents can be given opportunities to feel valued as members of the family, for example, making sure they have jobs such as dusting or folding towels when they wish to. These tasks may not be undertaken consistently, but that is irrelevant; when they are, appreciation will be shown by both sides, and people feel more part of life and have more sense of purpose. Carers see it as being important that there are 'real' activities that relate to people's past and the 'now' in which they are living: 'The sort of things they would have done before they came here'.

Activities can be promoted as a communal endeavour, but there also needs to be an awareness of the importance for some residents of being in company without participating: 'Some people like to sit in the background and just watch.'

There is a recurring theme when talking to residents about what they like to do, and it is a theme of expressed desire versus real desire, or perhaps of past and present tense being interchangeable. People will speak about something they enjoyed as though it were a current wish, but on exploration they have no desire to pursue it. Examples include the following exchanges, all with different interviewees:

> You said you missed doing your washing.
> Yes, I liked that, that was me.
> Would you like to do your own washing sometimes?
> Not sure I want to now!

> I used to do cooking.
> Would you like to do some cooking again?
> Some cooking – no!

> I love dancing, any dancing, love it.
> Would you like to do some?
> Good grief, no!

However, the last of these respondents said she would like to *watch* dancing, and this may be a clue on interpreting past activities into current enjoyment, as others echoed this:

> I like gardening, it was something I always used to do.

> Would you like to do some here, then?

> Not now, not now. I get pleasure from seeing people doing it.

This observation does not in any way suggest that there is no point in providing activities but rather that there should be no assumption that people are less happy if they do not join in. The important issue is to ensure the alternatives are available.

Staffing

One of the most critical implications of the observations made in this chapter, is that the demands on staff time are likely to be significantly greater in a dementia home, due to the different mode of listening required, the need to actively facilitate relationships, the slower pace of providing care in tune with residents and the more proactive role in liaising with families. However, designing the operation of the home to enable sufficient staff time to create a secure, 'family model' environment will yield very real benefits: more contented, interactive and healthy residents who are much less likely to require medication; staff who feel engaged and part of a community and relatives who may to an extent 'rediscover' their loved one and be more involved in their welfare. These benefits are primarily of an emotional and spiritual nature, but it cannot be assumed that for that reason they have no impact on the overall cost of dementia to public health provision.

A note on 'mixed' homes

While much dementia care is provided in specialist facilities, there are also a considerable number of homes with a mixture of residents, where only some are affected by dementia. It should also be borne in mind that some residents may not have dementia, but be affected by mental health problems, which can be at least as disruptive to the formation of 'family' relationships.

Broadly speaking, these mixed homes are of three types: small houses with residents who are in early stages of dementia, which may not have been formally diagnosed, but is recognised by others living with them; homes sufficiently large to have wings for dementia and non-dementia residents; and homes that were originally generalised, but have gradually become almost entirely dementia specialised. In this last case, a few of the original residents may still be there, occasionally because their partner has dementia.

The first type offers some advantages, in that residents can informally monitor and give feedback on those with dementia, can speak on their behalf about any problems, and can help with simple care, such as serving people at table. These are types of engagement that foster 'family' and a sense of purpose but this can only be taken so far before it becomes an imposition and a problem. Additionally, the mixture helps to keep the home linked into the local community, in which some of the residents are able to remain active.

The second model has the benefit of enabling transition into dementia care to be smoother, not least because the same staff may be serving all the wings, and already know people. However, as the number of people with dementia increases, this type of home runs the risk of the separate wings becoming increasingly mixed, until all are dominantly dementia care and other residents find it hard to cope with this.

The third type, where dementia care has 'taken over', can only succeed for all involved if there is a recognition of what is happening and good consultation with residents and their families. In some cases, making the house more dementia friendly is not always a problem, and in fact people may say that they would like to be helpful, and feel sympathetic to friends there who are becoming increasingly affected by dementia. In one home that had been converted, families of those 'left behind' were very worried, but the residents themselves all chose to stay. However, there may be strong resistance from some existing residents to making their home dementia friendly, perhaps because they dislike change or because they do not wish to be reminded of the condition, or most importantly feel they have not been involved in the process. It is important to note that changes can be subtle, and will in fact benefit everyone (especially those with conditions such as visual impairment) without having to implement change on a large, sudden or disruptive scale.

CHAPTER 7

THE RELATIONAL MODEL OF CARE

Introduction

Older people can thrive in residential or supported living homes: it need not be a 'second class' choice to be avoided until there is no option, but can provide a new lease of life, improved mental and physical health and as one resident I interviewed said to me, 'a little piece of heaven'. When older people and carers come together in supportive relationships, in a safe environment designed to favour the advantages of communal life and still provide privacy and individuality, the benefits to society cannot be overestimated.

The concept of 'mutual chaplaincy', where no one solely gives or receives but each enriches the other need not be just an aspiration, nor is it impossibly unaffordable. It does mean some adjustment in assumptions, mindset and policy and a willingness to put more public money into social care not only to reap subsequent savings in health care, but also to affirm our country as compassionate, civilised and forward thinking.

Paradoxes

Altering our mindset about the care of older people means recognising apparent paradoxes, so that myths and rarely explored assumptions can be seen for what they are, and cease to hold back planning and policy.

Independence is not in itself an ideal to be sought; humans are born to be interdependent and flourish through their relationships with others. Knowing there are other people around, especially if they are consistently present, generates security and confidence, both physically and emotionally. Autonomy is not the same as independence, and the more elements of control that people have over their lives, the more content and confident they are likely to be.

As people age, they are not necessarily (in fact rarely) better off in their 'own' home, whether they are single or a couple. This is a belief to which the ageing will cling until they have experienced an alternative, but sadly are being continually encouraged to hold on to. Thus, basically unsuitable premises are tinkered with to add various mobility and other aids as the person living there becomes increasingly isolated and lonely, and often fearful as well. Of course, in an ideal, close community this type of adaptation is worthwhile, so long as there are plenty of visitors, family and friends to give love and support. But the worst scenario is a decline into an almost total lack of company, a drift into reclusivity and a reliance on carers making rushed visits during which conversation is minimal.

Being on one's own does not represent independence in any real way, neither in terms of self-respect nor retaining a sense of self, but creates a high level of dependency on care that may not be there when most needed. The final indignity is the frail older person put to bed in the early evening during the final visit of the carer that day, wrapped in an adult nappy to see out the night.

The second apparent paradox is that life-enhancing care is not about 'giving' but lies in the interaction between giving and receiving, where both sides are playing both roles. Consider any healthy family or friendship and the truth of this is self-evident: the balance may change with time and circumstance, but a severe imbalance, where one person is consistently being looked after and the other continually drawn upon, cannot be good for either. If older people cannot give back, they become diminished.

It is therefore essential that however physically or mentally frail an older person may be, there are opportunities for them to play a role in family life and to feel their presence means something to others. Whether this is achieved through simple tasks, though conversation, through sharing information or memories, it must be factored in to daily life. This actually demands more, not less, staff time, as carers put thought into facilitating opportunities for contribution, but in return their own role is more positive and rewarding and residents become less needy and more fulfilled.

Physical and mental frailty does not mean that a person is frail in all ways: they may be spiritually robust, having a strong sense of self and the past, even if individual memories are fading. Staff can 'give' through respect for this individuality and through recognising and celebrating the offering that the older person brings to communal life.

The environment of the care home or housing can encourage and favour the creation of family bonds, but it must be a real home: if it looks lived-in, is very clean but maybe a bit messy, reflects the personalities of the people living and working there and avoids being beautiful but sterile, then it is probably a place where the inhabitants are living their lives rather than waiting to die.

The final paradox relates to investment and expenditure. Ensuring that our older people are not neglected or lonely, that they live as we would all wish to – knowing and being known – demands a high level of staff time and commitment. Until this can be viewed as an investment, the returns on which will include reduced staff stress, their improved retention rate, lower levels of illness and depression, fewer drug interventions, avoidance of crisis management and lower demand on the NHS, we will continue to repeat the current mistake of saving pennies now and spending pounds later.

The implications of establishing good relational care and mutual chaplaincy are nothing less than profound for policy and practice in residential care for older people. In summary these are:

- ensuring that people move to a care model that is rooted in a local community, such that existing relationships are retained and generations not separated, addressing loneliness and maintaining a sense of place and identity
- investing public money in social care, especially in staffing, to reduce healthcare expenditure on avoidable accidents and deterioration further down the line
- viewing older people as a national asset, not a cost to society
- encouraging a movement into residential care or supported housing before older people become very frail or dependent on home visits, so preserving their health, preventing rampant isolation and releasing their unsuitable accommodation as an asset into the pool of much-needed family housing.

New models of care

By 2036, the number of people aged over 85 in the UK will increase by 113.9 per cent (ONS 2016). Current government policy favours care at home and short-term support to maintain the 'independence' of older people, who themselves tend to prefer Independent Living Services (LaingBuisson 2015; (1) Table 4.10, (2) August 2010 – July 2016).

Nevertheless, the need for care home places is predicted to rise from 433,000 (in 2014) to 460,000 in 2020, with part of the impetus coming from the lack of places that currently delays, and will continue to delay, hospital discharge. The Local Government Association predicts that by 2035 the number of specialist care home places needed for older people will have risen by 400,000 units (LGA 2017).

Clearly, there is a need not only for greater provision, but also for a new vision if people are to fulfill their human potential for meaningful and rewarding life into old age. Interpreting the vision of 'family' for the twenty-first century clearly presents challenges, but more importantly it presents wonderful opportunities to re-think the role and place of older people in society, restoring rich relationships between them and between generations.

Already there are glimpses of this potential to be seen. Channel 4's *Old People's Home for 4-Year-Olds* set out to measure the impact of bringing the two age groups together with a day care arrangement for the children set in a retirement home, and revealed that the impact of the youngsters on those in their late 80s was very significant: after six weeks, the majority of metrics (such as cognition, mood and physical abilities) had improved markedly, and none of the elderly were depressed, including two who had been diagnosed with severe depression (Stewart and Johnson 2017).

In Deventer, Holland, students are living with older people in the Humanitas care home, exchanging the noise and cost of student halls for a wider range of ages in return for providing some assistance and two-way companionship. The think tank United for all Ages report published in January 2018 explores the concept in depth, and observes that such models are starting to be used more, and in the UK, in very recent times. For example, over the summer of 2017 the Cambridge Housing Society (CHS) set up a small-scale pilot Intergenerational Housing Project to provide accommodation for postgraduate students in one of its sheltered schemes at reduced rents, in return for volunteering and spending time with elderly residents. Existing residents were consulted on the project proposal on a collective and individual basis, with an overall positive response after some initial reticence. Three postgraduates were selected and trained in partnership with the Cambridge Hub, which engages Cambridge University students in practical local volunteering project. They recorded time spent on activities with residents, including befriending, running errands, preparing meals, film nights, trips and administrative activities such as meetings and student training in data protection, dementia awareness and so on. A methodology to measure developed by the project team – combining the Warwick-Edinburgh NHS wellbeing approach, with the Campaign to End Loneliness surveys – will measure impact on a quarterly basis against a baseline survey. In response to wide interest in the project from across housing and other sectors, CHS and the Cambridge Hub will be running briefings and workshops to share experience and learning from the initial six months.

At the other end of the age spectrum, some older people are taking arrangements into their own hands. For example, the Older Women's Co-housing Group comprising 26 older women from 51 to 88, has created the New Ground project in High Barnet, London. This is a community of individual apartments designed to provide a combination of privacy and mutual support, and based on the premise that everyone is willing to know and be known such that each can be respected and valued (Saul 2017).

One of the notable aspects of both these 'social experiments' is that they are based on similar observations to the findings of the Abbeyfield study: that facilitating formation of relationships which mirror family bonds is critical to wellbeing, and that older people must be given an active role in the society in which they live, within (but pushing at) the bounds of their ability. 'Care' is not about being done to, but about being helped to participate in the fullness of life.

Turning to look at very tangible interpretations of this axiom, and the findings on which it is based, Abbeyfield provides concrete examples. All its newer developments have been designed to reflect the factors observed to nurture human interaction in its older establishments, but taking advantage of fresh opportunities to design relationship-enabling environments.

In some cases, the charity has had the advantage of being able to build from scratch, and commission its architects to incorporate all the guidelines listed in Appendix A. In others, it has 'inherited' a building or an agreed plan, and had to adapt this to the best interpretation possible. An example of the latter is Hope Bank View in Silksworth, Sunderland, a new-build that comprises 75 extra care apartments with associated communal facilities.

Hope Bank View already had planning permission granted to a previous developer when it was bought by Abbeyfield, so it demanded some innovatory thinking to ensure it reflected the guidelines arising from the spirituality study, but this has been well achieved and the first residents arrived in late 2017.

One of the critical factors has been to ensure that the outside is brought in, such that residents remain connected to their community in terms of landscape as well as people, and vice versa. The buildings are close to countryside and lakes with views of the Tunstall hills, and to the existing residential community including shops, leisure centre, pubs and social clubs, with good public transport. This gave it many existing advantages in terms of connectivity, making it a more natural choice to fulfil the criteria.

Local artist Ian Potts was commissioned to provide a range of paintings and pictures reflecting the industrial heritage of Silksworth (a former mining village) and its surrounding landscape and coastline as well as the social history of Sunderland. Original pieces created for the project include winter gardens (now long gone but re-imagined as a mural in the treatment room), shopping (at Binns department store), the *Sunderland Echo* newspaper, and sport in the form of remembered days at the former Roker Park. The artwork is themed across floors for orientation and sense of place.

Ian will be facilitating residents to create their own artwork for the wall space outside their apartments in the form of 'Mackem Maps': community cartography based on the history of Sunderland. These will reflect their personal association with physical spaces in the area through drawings and paintings that meld symbolism and reality. If a resident chooses not to do a personal map but something else that speaks of who they are, they will be helped to create a space that is identifiably theirs. Similarly, the apartments, while having excellent basic facilities, have deliberately been left empty such that they can be personalised.

Inside, there is a main lounge with a TV, 'snug areas' close to a focal fireplace to encourage intimacy and provide privacy; dividing walls to create separate spaces for more versatility; an integral tea bar; and clever seating that also offers book case and shelf space. A separate quiet lounge without a TV also has a focal fireplace, various types of seating and tables, and is situated away from the lounge and dining room to ensure a restful environment that will encourage conversation. The dining room has views onto a large landscaped area and good natural light thanks to large windows and glass doors, and the front aspect of the building overlooks the car park and main road, keeping a sense of life going on outside and inside.

Outside, there has been room to accommodate generous gardens landscaped around the building to create different areas of interest with trees, shrubs, grass and seating easily accessed by handrails and level paths. There is space for residents to plant their own favourites. There is also a kitchen garden with sheds, raised beds and fruit trees where residents who wish to can grow and harvest food for their own meals and a sensory tranquillity garden in a quiet location with pergola seating and fragrant or tactile plants.

The entire development has been based on the findings of the research, designed to reflect all the environmental aspects that favour the formation of supportive relationships and of family bonds, with the management and staff offices central in the building and accessible to all, making for easy interaction and observation.

Other Abbeyfield developments, and particularly new-build where the architect has been able to design from scratch and cooperate closely with the in-house planning team, have all these features, as well as others that are very desirable. For example, Winnersh, a 60-bedroom specialist dementia care home near Reading, incorporates a number of lounges with different themes such as music, working life, travel, 'Gentlemen's Snug' and library, each with a focal point fireplace; and options to eat in the main dining room or at tables in the lounges which can be used for quiet dining. To facilitate circular walking, these areas and the personal accommodation are linked by corridors that have no dead ends. Large gardens with heated summerhouses and a spacious first floor terrace encourage residents to be outdoors, improving their mood and hence willingness to be outgoing and form connections.

CHAPTER 8

RETIREMENT CHOICES

It is the purpose of this chapter to explore what some of the issues and questions look like in relation to what choices people have around living together in older age and what possibly shapes those choices. We should acknowledge that retirement is a complex and changing reality for older people but that some of the choices made around housing happen at this stage of life.

Listening to others

ALAN

I am 72 and have absolutely no intention of retiring. I haven't any time for any of this modern nonsense of work–life balance. I thrive on the demands and stress of work. I think my wife wouldn't let me retire – she doesn't want me around the house and enjoys spending the money that comes from my business which I have built up over the last 50 years. My two sons are keen to take over, but they will have to wait. I believe I have experience, including the experience that comes from making many mistakes, and this experience can guide the business through the many demands of the modern, unpredictable market-place.

I am afraid that I am very impatient with my retired friends – all that golf and pointless foreign travel. Work is all I need and I am thankful for the chances that life has given me and for my ability to seize the opportunities of the moment.

MARJORIE

My husband died three years ago after a long illness. While I miss him, we had plenty of opportunity to say goodbye and put things in good order. I live in a large house in the suburbs of Birmingham, and I have a great passion for our garden and growing plants from seed. I have run the plant stall at the church summer fair for the last 28 years and appeared on television talking about my green fingers!

Well, it is time to be sensible. The house and garden are far too big and I need to move to something smaller and more economical. I have decided to move to a small retirement community to a two-bedroom bungalow. It is going to be quite a job sorting out all these years' accumulated clutter, but it has to be done. I enjoy the challenge of a task.

The advantages of such a community (about 120 people) are very clear. I will have to pay a maintenance charge, and they will look after all my needs. No more problems with roof tiles, plumbers or grass cutting. There will be new people to get to know and lots of different sorts of activities to join in. I am, of course, fortunate enough to be able to afford this kind of accommodation. The most important thing, for me, is that I shall be living in a place where, if I need extra support, I shall be able to access it. There is a residential and nursing unit on the site, which is a tremendous source of extra security. I am pretty stubborn but know when it is sensible to ask for help.

ALISON, JON, MARTHA, ROGER, KATE AND MARCIA

We have all been friends for some time and got to know each other through a variety of ways, mainly over our shared interest in art and music. We are in our 60s, and those of us with children are relatively free of responsibility. However, three of us have older relatives who are becoming increasingly dependent upon us. That is a concern.

After a great deal of thought we have decided to sell all of our houses and pool our resources in a common pot. We plan to move into a large house together in our retirement and run a small cooperative community. We are having great fun thinking through the aspects of how this will work. There are issues of both internal and external space. We also have to attend to the complex financial dimensions of the project and even have a plan when conflict happens. For us it is the perfect solution – a community of shared interest where we make decisions about what we need. We will 'buy in' a range of services as and when we need them, including care support. We want to work together to maintain and develop healthy ageing and to improve our quality of life. We also want, in our retirement, to offer something back to our community. Some of us will retain part-time paid work and others are planning to embark upon new avenues of growth and learning.

JOHN

I retired 20 years ago to what some of my friends regard as a life of idleness! I cannot tell you how liberated I felt from the burdens of work and responsibility. I sleep well, enjoy some gentle exercise, take an active interest in current affairs and read very widely. I cook and enjoy entertaining friends. I am a steady drinker and smoker. I am not especially introspective – I take each day as it comes and do my best to enjoy what these remaining days offer.

BARBARA

While I was looking forward to retirement my plans to move to the South Coast were changed by the premature death of my father. He was the main carer for my mother who has Alzheimer's disease. I stepped into his shoes and sold my house to move into the family home. I do my best to remain cheerful and positive but, as you can imagine, it isn't very easy. I have a great deal of support from social services and friends but the care is relentless in its demands. I do get opportunities for some space when my mother goes into respite care but sometimes find myself resentful that these 'golden retirement' years have been taken away from me by circumstances.

These five biographical reflections demonstrate clearly that it is impossible to generalise about older people and the diversity of perspectives that they bring. The following is a summary of a range of different reactions to retirement. These reactions, as we have noted, may well have a significant shaping effect on choices that are made in living arrangements for old age.

Rewards

- The sense of freedom which is absolutely wonderful.
- Being useful to my children and grandchildren and having the time to reconnect with them.
- Not having the burden of holding things together in my job.
- Being able to write letters and emails.
- Being free from some of the hassles of life.
- Being able to sleep whenever I want.
- Having the freedom to read new things and to discover new things.
- Being able to say the things that I want to!

Trials

- I never wanted to give up work and feel lost without it.
- Downsizing into a smaller home was tough.
- Saying goodbye to people I cared about.
- Unsure about why I should get out of bed in the morning!
- I wasn't quite sure that I was of worth any longer.
- Dealing with my ageing body and things slowing down.
- Concerned about having to spend my time entirely with older people.

Surprises

- Finding how tired I was when I stopped moving and sat still!

- Discovering all kinds of connections when I sat still and contemplated.
- Taking delight in small everyday things.
- A new sense of achievement at what my working life had done.
- Finding that I didn't have the slightest desire to go back to my work and role.
- Finding that I had more money than I expected to do the things I wanted to.

Factors affecting responses to retirement

The above responses, taken together with the case studies, illustrate a wide variety of reactions to retirement. This variation stems, in part at least, from differences in spirituality, in personal psychology, in life experience (and especially work experience) prior to retirement, in health, in family circumstances and other social networks and, not least, in the financial provision that it has been possible to make. Not only do these differences exist between different individuals but circumstances will change, and so will their relative significance, for the same person as they proceed further into old age. It is important therefore, in terms of pastoral care of those approaching retirement or those struggling to adjust to it, not to suppose or to suggest that there is a blueprint for a happy retirement which can simply be applied to every case. Sensitivity to the factors that may determine the nature of the retirement experience is essential. A good way of approaching retirement issues is to look at some of these factors in more detail, beginning with the more practical aspects.

Financial factors

All who go into retirement from full-time paid work will wish their standard of living to be maintained or at least kept at a level fairly close to that which they enjoyed while working. Some may find to their surprise that this is not as difficult as they had feared, particularly in the case of couples where both have occupational pensions as well as state pensions, but for others the new financial restraints may come as a rude awakening. Although, as businesses and advertisers have begun to realise, there are older people with money to spend (consider the rapid growth in cruising as a holiday activity) there are also many older people for whom poverty is a real issue. Age UK says that 1.9 million pensioners live in poverty, and that 7 per cent of pensioner couples and 24 per cent of single pensioners depend solely on state pensions. They also point out that there is an 'advice gap' whereby some people have too much income to be getting advice from welfare agencies but too little to be of interest to the financial services sector.

For those who are able to arrange it, having an adequate pension (company or private) and sound investment advice are two important factors in arriving at a financially worry-free retirement that will be maintained for many years to come. This ideal situation is more likely to be achieved if the planning starts at an early stage in life and is ongoing. It is for this reason that planning plays an important part in retirement education. The issues to be addressed might include some or all of the following:

- Adequate pension provision.
- Insurances.
- Ongoing investment security and strategy.
- Decisions on buying or renting property.
- Mortgage implications.
- Understanding of current taxation including capital gains tax.
- Inheritance tax planning and covenants.
- Sources for sound financial advice.
- Rights on change of employment (for example pension transfers).

Finally, it is worth saying before leaving this section that the ability to live happily within a certain level of income is not simply a matter of how big the figures are. It depends in part on having realistic expectations and the ability to come to terms with what is possible. There are people living on low incomes who perceive themselves to be rich and those living on incomes two or three times the size who bemoan their poverty. While it would not be true to say that it is 'all in the mind', perceptions of wealth and poverty do not correlate precisely to level of income.

Family and social circumstances

As the case studies and subsequent comments illustrate, retired people display a vast range of family and social circumstances. Retired people may be single or partnered, men or women. Those who are partnered may or may not have children or grandchildren. They may also have one or more parents still alive, needing varying degrees of attention; and they may or may not have brothers or sisters who can share the task. Other members of the family may live around the corner or across the world. The only certainty is that what it means to be a member of a family in retirement is likely to differ to some degree from what it meant when working. And, like every other aspect of retirement, this may be good or bad.

On the one hand many retired people welcome the opportunity to see more of their families in retirement, especially grandparents who delight in seeing their grandchildren growing up. On the other hand it is much harder in retirement to refuse any request that families may make and a third of grandparents provide the equivalent of three days a week childcare. One wonders how many of these made a positive choice to spend their retirement so heavily committed and consequently so restricted in pursuing the other possibilities which retirement might be thought to open up. Thus it can be that managing one's relationships with one's family becomes quite a major issue.

The factors that relate to families can also be relevant to other social networks. If you are fortunate enough to have many friends, retirement is an opportunity to spend more time with them, but if they are widely scattered around the country there may come a point where the amount of travel involved becomes a burden. Even if they live locally there is an issue about how much time you wish to spend in social activity and how much time you want to devote to more solitary pursuits like tending the garden or reading. Again these are matters which may require active management.

There is a further consideration in this. Many retired people take up activities which 'get them out of the house' and these may require varying degrees of commitment. If you join a choir or a musical group the other members will depend to some extent on your presence so it becomes a commitment. Likewise working one or two days a week in a charity shop or going to hear children read at the local primary school will involve agreeing to be there at set times. This may be exactly what some people need to provide structure to their lives and avoid that feeling of 'What do I have to get up for today?' On the other hand, it impinges on that freedom which many retired people consider to be the prime benefit of retirement. Here again psychological and temperamental differences are significant as some are capable of living with very little structure and others cannot do without it.

Health issues

Health – or lack of it – can obviously have a profound influence on a person's retirement prospects. For most people this may not be a major issue in the early years of retirement, though it obviously will for those forced to retire through ill health. Even in relatively early retirement, however, minor signs of physical decline may be in evidence, such as the need to take more frequent and longer rests when engaging in strenuous physical activity. As the years advance such limitations are liable to increase. Beyond the obvious advice about making healthy lifestyle choices and taking care not to fall, there is not a lot that anyone can do to forestall the diseases of old age, but again attitudes can be immensely important.

Life and work before retirement

The shape of retirement is bound to be heavily influenced by the nature of a person's life, and especially their work, prior to retirement, particularly in the first years when the contrast is most stark. This, of course, can cut both ways. Sadly, it seems that many people today can hardly wait to retire because of the pressure they are under at work yet they may still be surprised at how much they miss going out to work and the social contact that it provides. Conversely there are those who find it hard to imagine life without work but find the transition surprisingly easy once it happens. And of course it is possible for the same person to have ambivalent attitudes: on the one hand, 'Thank goodness I don't have to go to work any more' and on the other, 'Help! How am I going to fill my time?'

Which of these feelings is predominant is bound to depend to some extent on the part that work has played in a person's life previously. Those who have 'sold their souls to the company' will obviously be in a different position from those who have regarded their work as a nine-to-five occupation to pay the bills and whose 'real' life has always centred on their leisure interests.

There will also be clear differences between those, mainly in professional positions, who can continue doing some freelance work following their retirement or may use work-related skills in a voluntary capacity, and those whose work has to stop totally because it cannot be done outside a specialised environment, for example a car production line or a laboratory. There will be further differences in the extent to which work is missed because of the 'perks' it offered, ranging from indefinable elements such as social status and a sense of self-worth to very practical issues such as the access to a photocopier.

What many find is that the distinction between work and retirement is less sharp than they had imagined because certain aspects of retirement assume the characteristics of work. The only child who, in retirement, has to care for a parent with dementia will have less freedom than they ever had in their working life and their 'working hours' will be far longer. This is perhaps an extreme example but in every retirement situation there are those things that have to be done as well as those things we can choose to do. Nevertheless for most people retirement will bring an increase in choice and control, though that can in itself be problematic when there are too many choices and it becomes a major task to manage all the available options.

Personal psychology

It seems obvious that various aspects of personality will have a huge effect on the kind of retirement a person leads and how readily they will cope with different aspects of it, so it is surprising that these issues do not feature more prominently in the literature on ageing. A number of psychological profiling tools have been developed over the years and some of these are regularly used by human resources departments both in screening candidates applying for jobs and in mounting staff development programmes. It is undeniable that one's personality type, whatever the tools used to define it or the terms used to describe it, is highly influential in the way one relates to other people and in the way one approaches a task. It is therefore inevitable that it will be a significant influence in how people choose to shape their retirement.

At a most obvious level the widely recognised distinction between introverts and extroverts will come into play. Those who depend on being with others to bring them alive will surely seek out the company of others and will want to engage in a range of social activities while those who are more self-sufficient may be happy to 'do their own thing'. This is not, of course, an absolute distinction but a matter of balance. Introverts are not necessarily averse to company nor extroverts incapable of sitting quietly by themselves for a while, but their differences in personality will be a factor in shaping their choices.

Other kinds of personality trait may be equally influential, for example the distinction already mentioned between those who need everything to be 'cut and dried' and those who are happy to 'go with the flow'. Certain aspects of ageing can be particularly trying for those who like to be in control and have been accustomed to being in control throughout their lives. How does such a person cope when they contract an illness which means that they cannot tell from one day to the next what they might be capable of doing? How do they learn to 'go with the flow' when all their instincts favour having a plan?

Personality factors may be particularly important in decisions about accommodation when it becomes increasingly difficult for a single person or a surviving partner to remain in the house they have lived in for many years. Many surveys have shown that one of the losses people living on their own feel most keenly is the loss of community. In many ways it would seem that the obvious solution for this would be a move to a residential home, especially as one of the well-known personality profiling tools claims that extroverts outnumber introverts three to one. But what of the 25 per cent who show varying degrees of introversion and especially the smaller percentage who are highly introverted? Even if all care homes were as good as the best, such a person might find living in residential care very difficult to bear and it might be more appropriate in such a case to try to continue to support him or her in their own home, however difficult this may be.

Given that personality differences seem not to be widely discussed as an issue in retirement it may be important to pay particular attention to this aspect.

CONCLUSION

In this conclusion, we want to identify and elaborate eight key components for future consideration, research and development. The debate must go on as we work together to commit ourselves to developing excellence for new models or structures of care for living together in old age.

These components, which must find expression in structures of care, overlap with each other but should include: the integrated nature of a model of care; the empowerment of older people; the reciprocal nature of relationships between those giving and those receiving care; the provision of good staff support; a physical environment that fosters connectivity and community; the emphasis on equality; a commitment to excellence and an awareness of the art of embracing and managing ambiguity.

An integrated model of care

In the future it could be that homes for older people living together might act as a hub for the delivery of a wide range of interlocking services. These could include informal drop-in services, counselling and pastoral care, support groups especially for those living with dementia, day care, complementary and creative therapies, training programmes, home support and respite alongside convalescent and terminal care. What we have learnt from this study is that there needs to be a shared commitment to function as a home from home, where people in a particular community can build a network of relationships developed over a period of time. This interconnectivity might be able to meet different needs at different stages of the ageing process and thereby ensure that various services are delivered in a coordinated way and relationships are not disrupted.

It also means that people engaged in delivering care alongside older people can develop their own network of respectful relationships across professional boundaries, doctors with complementary therapists, care workers with nurses and home support workers, professionals with volunteers, counsellors with advice workers or trainers, and so on.

Traditionally, care has tended to be fragmented in its delivery, inconsistent in its quality and for some people somewhat inaccessible, with different disciplines disconnected or even polarised. In this culture there is an opportunity to develop a holistic and integrated approach.

The empowerment of older people

We must no longer persist in perpetuating an ageism, which has all the potential and capacity to marginalise older people. While a growing number of older people presenting complex social, health and economic needs is undoubtedly challenging, this is also an opportunity for transformation. An important component of relational care therefore is a clear focus on the possibility for each recipient of personal growth, change and transformation. It has the potential to release energy and creativity so that we can all live and learn together across the generations.

Translated into practice this means seeing and treating an older person receiving care as central, and as far as possible autonomous, and as much in charge of the decision-making process as they wish to be. This means that we should work with older people rather than for older people. It will certainly reconstruct our relationship to providing time and attention, with an imperative to resource presence and engagement in such a way as to foster the creation of relationships in the process of delivering care and support. During care-giving an older person's intuitive, spiritual and emotional life can be released and enabled.

The most obvious way that this approach to empowerment can be facilitated is to acknowledge an explicit commitment to consulting older people using services on all major matters of policy.

The reciprocal nature of relationships between those providing and those receiving care

Those reading this book who are involved in the organisation and delivery of services to older people will be more than aware of the day-to-day pressure of that work: this is often an undervalued and under-resourced dimension of our social care system. However, it is easy to forget the relationship between those who deliver care and those who receive it. In all real relationships, there must be true reciprocity without which it may not be possible for such relationships to become real and mutually empowering.

In real relationships both parties give and receive; love each other, fall out and sometimes disagree; struggle and negotiate with each other in working together towards honesty. There is a sense in which those who work with older people open themselves up to the losses and changes that are inevitable when people die or move on. Organisations providing care need to offer the opportunity to develop a reciprocity that is authentic and relational, and to ensure that managers can support their staff in times of loss, whilst being supported themselves. Without this approach, there is a risk that care, eventually, becomes ineffective or even inhumane.

The provision of good staff support

If new structures of care are to be nurtured and developed the fourth element of effectiveness and creativity will therefore be support. The point is simple: we all have needs to be met, and it is important as care-givers to be aware of what those needs are. Otherwise, it is easy to confuse the meeting of our own needs with the care we give.

This will mean an investment by the organisation staff time, to care for not only residents but also each other. Facilitating this on-the-ground 'mutual chaplaincy' needs the back up of a formal support system so creating a climate in which people are reassured they can access intelligent, effective informal support at moments of crisis, and in which the meeting of people's emotional and spiritual needs is seen as a healthy and routine activity.

A physical environment that fosters connectivity

An investment in staff – their recruitment, time and support – must go hand in hand with an investment in the care home or supported housing, ensuring it has the features that foster the formation of good relationships and the creation of family, such that those living there are working with, not against, their environment. This is beneficial to all involved, as the investment will provide future savings in terms of contentment, retention, lower maintenance and improved wellbeing.

The emphasis on equality

We continue to live in an unequal and sometimes oppressive society, in which economic inequity, classism, racism, sexism and ageism see to it that equality of opportunity is far from our day-to-day reality. The extent to which an organisation or agency has to relate to mainstream society, and is dependent upon it for its funding, means it is bound to become to some extent an oppressive microcosm of that society.

Those who organise themselves for providing places where older people can live together therefore have a unique opportunity to address the issue of equality within new structures of care.

Is it therefore too much to expect that the issue of equality might embed itself through a strong commitment to face the issue in and through the structures of care? This commitment could be addressed through the development of organisational policies, operational procedures, public relations, consciousness-raising, training and importantly staff recruitment. Unless this awareness of the reality of oppression, and of its structural and personal consequences, is made explicit as part of the context in which care is delivered, there is a potential for any organisation to become rapidly unsafe for groups of people who need its services.

It is worth here adding a word about language. Many of our traditional models of care derive from the time when patriarchal values were assumed, and when our understanding of the framework of oppression particularly in the area of ageism was very limited. Much of the traditional language of care around older people reflects this: it can be dehumanising and alienate older people. Elderly, old dear, sufferer, patient, client and many other words may come readily but in fact reinforce the profound marginalisation already being experienced by those people who need care.

The commitment to excellence

Far too often we have settled for second best in many areas of old age care. In this book we have seen centres of care that are committed to excellence, and we hope that there might be a renewal of aspiration in those who plan for the provision of places where people can live together in old age.

The old adage tells us that if a job's worth doing it's worth doing well and that belief needs strengthening within this area of work. However, we need also to attend to the outcome of care in this commitment to excellence.

The roots of this may well be found within ourselves as we articulate with honesty what we would want for ourselves in living with old age.

The art of managing ambiguity

When ageing is described as both blessing and burden there is embedded in the assertion an ambiguity. The frailties of old age may indeed offer positive opportunity and a relational model of care proposes a foundation for places that can be focused on living well, on freedom and on transformation. If they are truly homes, then they must be places where people can not only live well but also die well.

In the journey of old age, ambiguities abound and often our fear makes us long for certainty where there is none.

What would our society look like if places of care for older people became centres of excellence offering a model of care for every stage or need within each generation? How do we work together to nurture models of best practice where people can access dependable, professional and engaged services? How can we nurture a model of ageing which is focused on living well, and on indefinable, intangible, serious issues like love, hope and empowerment? What is the potential for us to commit ourselves to such spiritual matters that touch all our lives, as we attempt to eliminate isolation through tackling inequality and injustice? Are we willing to embrace change and to develop and nurture systems of support, recognising healing, health, vulnerability, frailty and death?

It may well be that in holding together the tensions and ambiguities – the objective response to things as they are, or are perceived to be, with these other more subjective and mysterious elements – in the day-to-day struggle, there lies the possibility and promise of transformation for the quality of life for older adults. It may even be that it is only in a climate where everyone is engaged in this struggle, with integrity and with love, that real flourishing can take place.

APPENDIX A

What to look for in a home

When seeking the best possible home to suit a loved one, it is all too easy to assess the accommodation and services from your own point of view rather than that of your relative. Of course, you know more about your loved one's preferences, way of life and what most matters to them than probably anyone else, but it is possible to get 'seduced' by seeing somewhere that appears luxurious, beautifully decorated, well appointed and so on – all the aspects that may make it attractive if you were looking for a good hotel.

However, families don't live in hotels, they live in homes. If family-style bonds are going to form, helping your loved one to thrive and feel that life offers pleasure and meaning, then you need to be alert to a number of factors that may not have been top of your mind.

Also, ideally, you need to arrange for your relative to stay for a short break, or at least visit for lunches or days, before making a commitment. It is important not to leave it too late. Moving before an older person has become very frail, and before they have no choice left, is much more positive and likely to lead to a better outcome.

These are some of the things to consider:

Location

- Is the home close to a community of which your relative has been part?
- Can they still have contact with friends, clubs, local church and so on?

- If they are moving to be close to you, do consider how much time you will have available to visit them, and what they may lose as well as gain from the move to a new locality.

Accommodation: personal

- Is their bedroom or flat an area that can be personalised, or is it already decorated in a 'hotel' style? How much help will the resident be given in personalising it, for example having their own furniture, hanging photos or paintings on the walls? Can it be made to feel light and bright, and welcoming to others? Remember this will be your relative's home, not just a bedroom.
- Is there more than one window, and what are the views like? Will they be able to see people and movement, such as a street or park?
- Can the room be made secure from other residents wandering in (especially in a 'mixed dementia' home)?
- Are there any restrictions about making drinks or storing food in the room?

Accommodation: communal

- What are the communal rooms like? Is there a variety of smaller, quiet rooms for conversation? Do they have focal points such as a fireplace (not TV) that people can sit around?
- Are communal areas decorated to give each a 'character' so the environment is not bland?
- Are there residents' belongings in the communal areas, such as photos or paintings that mean something to them and a safe place to display people's possessions such as ornaments?
- If there is a main lounge, is it dominated by a TV? Are chairs arranged to promote interaction?
- Are communal rooms being used, in particular for conversation or activity, or are they quiet and empty?

- Is there a piano, and if so, is it in an area that encourages people to gather round?
- Does the dining room feel like a family area or a restaurant? Does it have plenty of windows?
- What are the arrangements for the kitchen – can the cook easily talk to residents so that they feel part of the food preparation if they wish to?
- Is there a garden room?
- Are the gardens easy to access and walk round? Do they have areas of different character?
- If there is a summerhouse, is it heated in the winter, and does it have a drink-making station?
- Are the corridors long and straight or designed to permit 'circular walks'? Do they have places to sit, niches with ornaments or displays, good lighting?

Food and mealtimes

- Is there at least one obligatory communal mealtime, either lunch or dinner?
- Are there other opportunities to share food, for example coffee mornings, tea times and do the carers join in to help build family bonds?
- How are the menus decided and what input do residents have?
- Is all food freshly prepared by a cook who is part of the 'family' and talks to residents?
- Are residents able to help if they want, for example with laying tables, making cakes?
- Are there 'drinks stations' or easy access to hot drinks whenever someone wants one?

Personal care

- How will your relative be looked after: by an allocated lead carer? A team? What will be the role of the House Manager?
- Does the House Manager appear to know all the residents well? Are they sitting chatting with them, or based in an office when you visit?
- What is the extent of the assistance available, and how flexible is it?
- How is personal care such as dressing, washing, toileting and help with moving around offered? Are people being respected when care is given? (It is worth staying in the home for some time to watch the interactions and see whether people feel relaxed and talk to one another when care is bring provided, or whether it is at all rushed or impersonal.)
- How are personal effects, especially clothes, looked after? Do residents look like they have dressed with care?

APPENDIX B

Impact on Environmental Design

As is clear from the observations detailed in this book, it is almost impossible to separate out the physical, emotional and spiritual environments, as they are so closely inter-related in their effects on wellbeing and their impact on one another. However, working closely with the Abbeyfield Development department and an architect with considerable experience of designing for care (independent living, extra care and residential care), a guideline document reflecting the impact of the research on the built environment was developed to embody each critical finding. The criteria it proposes have been carefully interpreted and will be followed in new Abbeyfield developments, as described in the examples given in Chapter 7. The research findings are reflected throughout the full, confidential document that will be issued to architects and main contractors, but with Abbeyfield's permission, an extract is reproduced below.

The Abbeyfield Spirituality Design Guidelines

Spirituality is an important factor within an Abbeyfield retirement scheme and adds to the overall wellbeing and enjoyment of the building by residents, visitors and staff alike. Spirituality is therefore a key consideration when identifying design standards, which is reflected in many of the design principles set out in this document, and throughout the Design Guide.

The following are considered to be the 'top 10' spirituality design requirements to be incorporated into Abbeyfield's retirement living projects:

1. To provide residents with variety and choice, at least two communal rooms (i.e. lounge and dining room) should be provided in small homes (40 units), and at least three in larger homes (60 units plus).
2. A 'garden' room, such as an orangery or conservatory, should be considered.
3. Each apartment should have access to a personal, outdoor space in the form of a balcony or terrace.
4. A focal point should be provided in all lounges, such as a real fire (or very good simulation), with a large welcoming fireplace/mantelpiece to invite people to sit and interact.
5. A sheltered outdoor space, such as a summerhouse, should be provided within the garden to encourage residents to maximise their time within the garden.
6. There should be some variation in style of apartments including layout and interior decoration to promote choice.
7. Dining rooms should be designed to maximise natural light with attractive views out into the garden and beyond to ensure a pleasant dining experience for residents and visitors, with plenty of light for the visually impaired.
8. The lounge should be family oriented, with access to safe drinks preparation by occupants.
9. Staff should have a 'peaceful' retreat away from residents to enjoy their breaks.
10. Whilst efficient, long straight corridors should be avoided wherever possible to ensure that the circulation spaces do not feel institutional.

Bibliography

Age UK (2014) 'Evidence Review: Loneliness in Later Life.' Accessed 5 March 2018 at https://www.ageuk.org.uk/globalassets/age-uk/documents/reports-and-publications/reports-and-briefings/health--wellbeing/rb_june15_lonelines_in_later_life_evidence_review.pdf

Aitchley, R. (2009) *Spirituality and Ageing*. Baltimore, MD: Johns Hopkins University Press.

Albans, K. and Johnson, M. (eds) (2013) *God, Me and Being Very Old: Stories and Spirituality in Later Life*. London: SCM Press.

Alzheimer's Society (2015) 'Walking About.' Factsheet 501LP.

Arking, R. (2006) *The Biology of Ageing: Observations and Principles*. Oxford: Oxford University Press.

Athill, D. (2008) *Somewhere Towards the End*. London: Granta.

Bateson, M.C. (1989) *Composing a Life*. New York: Grove Press.

Bateson, M.C. (2010) *Composing a Further Life: The Age of Active Wisdom*. New York, NY: Vintage Books.

Bauman, Z. (1992) *Mortality, Immortality and Other Life Strategies*. Cambridge: Polity Press.

Bengston, V.L., Gans, D., Putney, N.M. and Silverstein, M. (2009) *Handbook of Theories of Ageing*. New York, NY: Springer Verlag.

Board for Social Responsibility (1990) *Ageing*. London: Church of England.

Bytheway, B. (1995) *Ageism*. Buckingham: Open University Press.

Bytheway, B. (2011) *Age and Time in Unmasking Age*. Bristol: Policy Press.

Cassidy, S. (1989) *Sharing the Darkness: The Spirituality of Caring*. London: DLT.

Chittister, J.D. (2008) *The Gift of Years*. London: Darton, Longman & Todd.

Coleman, P. (2011) Belief and Ageing: Spiritual Pathways in Later Life. Bristol: Policy Press.

Collins, J. (1953) *The Mind of Kirkegaard*. Princeton, NJ: Princeton University Press.

Cottam, H. (2013) *Today*. London: BBC Radio 4, 18 December 2013.

Cottam, H. and Dillon, C. (2014) *Learning from London Circle*. London: Participle.

Commission on Funding of Care and Support (2011) *Fairer Care Funding: The Report of the Commission on Funding of Care and Support*. Accessed on 09/01/2018 at http://webarchive.nationalarchives.gov.uk/20130221130239/http://dilnotcommission.dh.gov.uk

Counsel and Care (1995) *Last Rights: A Study of How Death and Dying are Handled in Residential Care and Nursing Homes*. London: Counsel and Care.

Croucher, K. and Bevan, M. (2012) *Promoting Supportive Relationships in Housing with Care*. York: Joseph Rowntree Foundation.

Culliford, L. (2015) *Much Ado about Something: A Vision of Christian Maturity*. London: SPCK.

Frawley, D. (1990) *The River of Heaven: Hindu and Vedic Knowledge for the Modern Age*. Twin Lakes: Lotus Press.

Glendenning, F. (ed.) (2000) *Teaching and Learning in Later Life: Theoretical Implications*. Aldershot: Ashgate.

Gordon, T. (1997) 'Clearing the dark corners of the mental attic.' *Professional Social Work*, January 1997.

Hauerwas, S., Stoneking, C.B., Meador, K.G. and Cloutier, D. (eds) (2003) *Growing Old in Christ*. Grand Rapids, MI: William B. Eerdmans.

Jewell, A. (ed.) (1999) *Spirituality and Ageing*. London: Jessica Kingsley Publishers.

Jewell, A. (ed.) (2001) *Older People and the Church*. Peterborough: Methodist Publishing House.

Jewell, A. (ed.) (2004) *Ageing, Spirituality and Well-being*. London: Jessica Kingsley Publishers.

Killick, J. (2013) *Dementia Positive: A Handbook Based on Lived Experiences*. Edinburgh: Luath Press.

Kirkwood, T.B.L. (1999) *Time of Our Lives: The Science of Human Ageing*. London: Weidenfeld & Nicolson.

LaingBuisson (2015) *Care of Older People, UK Market Report*, 27th edn, September. London: LaingBuisson.

Laslett, P. (1996) *Fresh Map of Life: The Emergence of the Third Age*. London: Macmillan.

LGA (2017) '"Residential revolution" needed for England's ageing population, says LGA.' *Housing Our Ageing Population*. London: Local Government Association, ref 5.17. Accessed 5 March 2018 at https://www.local.gov.uk/about/news/residential-revolution-needed-englands-ageing-population-says-lga

Lyon, K.B. (1985) *Toward a Practical Theology of Aging*. Philadelphia, PA: Fortress Press.

MacKinlay, E. (2001) *The Spiritual Dimension of Ageing*. London: Jessica Kingsley Publishers.

MacKinlay, E. (2006) *Spiritual Growth and Care in the Fourth Age*. London: Jessica Kingsley Publishers.

McSherry, W. (2006) *Making Sense of Spirituality in Nursing and Health Care Practice*. London: Jessica Kingsley Publishers.

Merchant, R. (2003) *Pioneering the Third Age: The Church in an Ageing Population*. Exeter: Paternoster Press.

Moffitt, L. (1996) 'Helping to recreate a personal sacred space.' *Journal of Dementia Care*, 4, 3.

Morgan, K. (ed.) (1992) *Gerontology: Responding to an Ageing Society*. London: Jessica Kingsley Publishers.

Nouwen, H. (2003) *The Return of the Prodigal Son*. London: DLT, p.72.

O'Brien, E. (2011) *Spirituality in Nursing: Standing on Holy Ground*. Sudbury, MA: Jones and Bartlett.

ONS (Office for National Statistics) (2016) 'Estimates of the very old (including centenarians), UK: 2002 to 2015.' London: Office for National Statistics.

Palmore, E.B., Branch, L.G. and Harris, D.K. (eds) (2005) *Encyclopedia of Ageism*. Binghamton, NY: Haworth Pastoral Press.

Pattison, S. (2001) 'Dumbing Down the Spirit.' In H. Orchard (ed.) *Spirituality in Health Care Contexts*. London: Jessica Kingsley Publishers.

Peace, S. and Holland, C. (eds) (2001) *Inclusive Housing in an Ageing Society*. Bristol: The Policy Press.

Peberdy, A. (1993) 'Spiritual Care of Dying People.' In D. Dickenson and M. Johnson (eds) *Death, Dying and Bereavement*. London: Sage.

Saul, H. (2017) 'How the older women who built their own co-housing community found their first year together.' *inews*, 19 October 2017.

Saunders, C. (2005) *Watch with Me: Inspiration for a Life in Hospice Care*. Lancaster: Observatory Publications.

Shaw, G.B. (1939) *Back to Methuselah*. London: Penguin Books.

Slater, R. (1995) *Psychology of Growing Old*. Buckingham: Open University Press.

Stewart, M. and Johnson, M. (2017) 'What happened when we introduced four-year-olds to an old people's home.' *The Conversation*. Accessed 5 March 2018 at https://theconversation.com/what-happened-when-we-introduced-four-year-olds-to-an-old-peoples-home-82164

Tanner, D. (2010) *Managing the Ageing Experience: Learning from Older People*. Bristol: The Policy Press.

United for All Ages (2017) *A Country for all ages: Ending age apartheid in Brexit Britain*. Accessed on 09/01/2018 at http://unitedforallages.com/wp-content/uploads/2017/01/A-Country-for-All-Ages-January-2017.pdf

United for all Ages (2018) 'Mixing Matters.' Accessed 5 March 2018 at http://unitedforallages.com/wp-content/uploads/2018/01/Mixing-Matters-United-for-All-Ages-paper-Jan-2018-.pdf

University of Exeter (2014) 'Study reveals how gardens could help dementia care.' Accessed on 08/01/2018 at www.exeter.ac.uk/news/featurednews/title_401848_en.html

Wainwright, D. (2001) *Being Rather Than Doing*. Occasional paper 13. Northampton: CCOA.

Walker, A. (ed.) (2014) *The New Science of Ageing*. Bristol: Policy Press.

Warnes, A. (ed.) (2000) *Care Services for Later Life*. London: Jessica Kingsley Publishers.

Whear, R., Thompson Coon, J., Bethel, A., Abbott, R., Stein, K. and Garside, R. (2014) 'What is the impact of using outdoor spaces such as gardens on the physical and mental well-being of those with dementia? A systematic review of quantitative and qualitative evidence.' *The Journal of Post-Acute and Long-term Care Medicine 15*, 10, 697–705.

Wildlife Trust (2017) *Natural World*, Summer, pp.5–8.

Withnall, A., McGivney, V. and Soulsby, J. (2004) *Older People Learning: Myths and Realities*. Leicester: Niace with the UK Department for Education and Skills.

Woodward, J. (2005) *Befriending Death*. London: SPCK.

Woodward, J. (2008) *Valuing Age: Pastoral Ministry with Older People*. London: SPCK.

Young, M. and Schuller, T. (1991) *Life after Work: The Arrival of the Ageless Society*. London: HarperCollins.

Useful Organisations and Websites

Care providers

The CareGuide website (https://ukcareguide.co.uk) will provide a database of providers of housing and care in your area.

Amongst the national providers (of which the authors are aware) look at:

Abbeyfield
https://www.abbeyfield.com

Anchor
www.anchor.org.uk

MHA
www.mha.org.uk

McCarthy and Stone
https://www.mccarthyandstone.co.uk

Sunrise Living
www.sunrise-care.co.uk

Star and Garter Homes
https://starandgarter.org/our-homes

The Almshouse Association
www.almshouses.org

The Joseph Rowntree Trust (see especially the development at Hartrigg Oaks)
https://www.jrht.org.uk/community/hartrigg-oaks-york

Advice and support

Action on Elder Abuse

Aims to prevent abuse by raising awareness, encouraging education, promoting research and collecting and disseminating information.

Astral House
1268 London Road
London SW16 4ER
Tel: 020 8765 7000
Helpline: 0808 808 8141
Website: www.elderabuse.org.uk

Alzheimer's Society

Provides information and local support to help people with dementia and their carers cope with the day-to-day realities of dementia. It funds research and campaigns on issues connected with dementia.

Devon House
58 St Katharine's Way
London E1W 1JX
Tel: 020 7423 3500
Helpline: 0845 300 0336
Website: www.alzheimers.org.uk

Carers UK

Improves carers' lives through research, information, provision of services and campaigning

20–25 Glasshouse Yard
London EC1A 4JT
Tel: 020 7490 8818
Helpline: 0808 808 7777
Website: www.carersuk.org

Cinnamon Trust

A specialist national charity for older people and their pets. Has a register of pet-friendly care homes.

10 Market Square
Hale
Cornwall TR27 4HE

Tel: 01736 757900
Website: www.cinnamon.org.uk

Cruse Bereavement Care

Promotes the wellbeing of bereaved people, providing counselling and support.

PO Box 800
Richmond
Surrey TW9 1RG
Tel: 020 8939 9530
Helpline: 0844 477 9400
Website: www.crusebereavementcare.org.uk

Elderly Accommodation Counsel

Helps older people to make decisions about housing and support needs. Keeps registers of housing with care and care homes.

3rd Floor
89 Albert Embankment
London SE1 7PT
Tel: 020 7820 1343
Website: www.housingcare.org

National Association of Citizens Advice Bureaux

Provides free advice from over 300 locations which helps people resolve their legal, financial and other problems.

Myddleton House
115–123 Pentonville Road
London N1 9LZ
Tel: 0845 126 4264
Website: www.citizensadvice.org.uk

Princess Royal Trust for Carers

Provides comprehensive care support services through an independently managed network of 129 Carers Centres.

142 Minories
London EC3N 1LB
Tel: 020 7480 7788
Website: www.carers.org

Relatives and Residents Association

Supports older people finding or living in care homes and their families and friends.

24 The Ivories
6–18 Northampton Street
London N1 2HY
Tel: 020 7359 8148
Helpline: 020 7359 8136
Website: www.relres.org

University of the Third Age

A network of self-help, self-managed lifelong learning cooperatives for older people.

Unit 3, Carpenters Court
4a Lewes Road
Bromley BR1 2RN
Tel: 020 8466 6139
Website: www.u3a.org.uk

Policy organisations

Age UK England

A national charitable movement concerned with the needs and aspirations of older people. Produces an excellent series of information leaflets on matters of concern to older people.

Astral House
1268 London Road
London SW16 4ER
Tel: 020 8765 7000
Website: https://www.ageuk.org.uk

The British Society of Gerontology

Aims to promote the understanding of ageing and later life through research and communication between different disciplines.

See website for current officers' contact details:

Website: www.britishgerontology.org

Centre for Policy on Ageing
Focuses on enhancing the exchange of knowledge and information to keep policy makers, practitioners and researchers better informed about current issues affecting older people.

25–31 Ironmonger Row
London EC1V 3QP
Tel: 020 7553 6500
Website: www.cpa.org.uk

The King's Fund
An independent charitable foundation working for better health, especially in London. It is involved in research, policy analysis and development and has an important library which is open to the public.

11–13 Cavendish Square
London W1G 0AN
Tel: 020 7307 2400
Website: www.kingsfund.org.uk

National Care Forum
Represents the views of not-for-profit health and social care organisations that provide care services for older people.

3 The Quadrant
Coventry CV1 2DY
Tel: 0247 624 3619
Website: www.nationalcareforum.org.uk

Participle Community Links
Instigated the 'Circle' care system based on using social media. This is now a legacy website.

Website: www.participle.net

Social Care Institute for Excellence
Collects, synthesises and disseminates knowledge about what works in social care.

Goldings House
2 Hay's Lane
London SE1 2HB
Tel: 020 7098 6840
Website: www.scie.org.uk

United for all Ages

A think tank established in 2010.

Tel: 01692 650816
Website: unitedforallages.com

Church-related organisations

Christian Council on Ageing

Aims to assist churches and individual Christians to respond to the pastoral needs of older people.

Website: www.ccoa.org.uk

Faith in Older People

Aims to celebrate the lives of older people and support them in their various needs by using a network provided by faith communities throughout Scotland and offering support and training to lay and ordained members of all faith communities.

21a Grosvenor Crescent
Edinburgh EH12 5EL
Tel: 0131 364 7981
Website: www.faithinolderpeople.org.uk

MHA Care Group

Provides care, housing and support services for older people throughout Britain and promotes the importance of the spiritual needs of older people.

Epworth House
Stuart Street
Derby DE1 2EQ
Tel: 01332 296200
Website: www.mha.org.uk

Parche (Pastoral Action in Residential Care Homes for the Elderly)

An ecumenical project which aims to meet the spiritual needs of older people in residential care in Eastbourne through providing regular services and visits in care homes and retirement housing schemes.

St Elizabeth's Church Centre
268 Victoria Drive
Eastbourne BN20 8QX
Tel: 01323 438527
Website: www.parche.org.uk

Government Departments

Department for Work and Pensions

Responsible for benefits and the Government welfare reform agenda.

The Adelphi
1–11 John Adam Street
London WC2N 6HT
Tel: 020 7712 2171
Website: www.dwp.gov.uk

Department of Health

Improves health and wellbeing and promotes health and social care policy.

Richmond House
79 Whitehall
London SW1A 2NS
Tel: 020 7210 4850
Website: www.dh.gov.uk

Index

Professor James Woodward is principal of Sarum College and a visiting professor of Theology at the University of Winchester. He is a teacher and writer of pastoral and practical theology. He is passionate about learning, change and growth that might be empowered through our careful engagement with people and the questions that shape human wellbeing.

As an Anglican priest his concerns have been formed by the diversity of contexts within which he has worked, including pastoral work with people at various stages of their living and dying; health and social care in acute and primary care settings; organisational development theological education and inter-professional collaboration on ethics.

For the last thirty years, he has had a particular interest in the nature of age and the place of older people in society. Presently he is writing on theological reflection and researching the potential of narratology to nurture human flourishing.

For further information about his work visit: www.jameswoodward.info

Jenny Kartupelis started her career in public relations, establishing an award-winning business. In 1998 her focus moved to interfaith relations, and she was instrumental in setting up the East of England Faiths Council, of which she became director. During the lifetime of the Council, Jenny conducted research and surveys and wrote a number of guidance documents on good practice. She was appointed to the DCLG faith advisory panel by the Secretary of State for Communities and was awarded the MBE for services to interfaith relations.

She has been commissioned to undertake extensive survey work by charities and the public sector, resulting in changes of practice and policy; her commission by The Abbeyfield Society led to the findings that have in part inspired this book, as well as having a significant impact on the client's own offering.

Jenny provides strategic and development advice to The World Congress of Faiths; is a Director of Faith in Society Ltd.; and a Visiting Fellow of Goldsmiths London University.